Pray Like Jesus

How to Pray When You're Not Sure What to Say

Ricky Smith, Samuel Thomas, Frank Bowden

Published by Impact Media, Columbus, GA

Impact Media
7556 Old Moon Road
Columbus, GA 31909 USA
www.calvaryga.com

Book Editing: Readable Reach
readablereachbooks.com

Cover Design: Laura Atterbury, Calvary Baptist Church

Pray Like Jesus: How to Pray When You're Not Sure What to Say -- 1st ed.

ISBN: 978-1-7359462-1-4

This book is dedicated to the orphans and widows of India who are cared for by the ongoing ministry of Hopegivers International.

CONTENTS

INTRODUCTION

You have been given the greatest gift anyone could possibly imagine. It is a gift that brings wisdom, comfort, encouragement, joy, peace, and total transformation.

That gift is access to God Himself in prayer!

No other faith system has a God who is personal, who listens, who acts on our behalf, who loves us, and who is fully good. The God of Christianity, the true God, is all of those things, and He not only *listens* to us and responds to our prayers; He came here among us as a human being and taught us *how* to pray!

Jesus Christ, God Himself, gave a model for how to pray when His disciples asked Him to teach them. We call this the Lord's Prayer, and it is recorded for us in the Bible.

Have you ever stopped to talk to God and had no idea where to start or what to say? Do you ever wonder if He hears you? Do you wonder if He understands what you are going through? Well, rest assured that Jesus knows exactly what you are going through, since He lived a life here as one of us, and His resurrection from the dead proves that His words are trustworthy.

As a trustworthy guide and part of the Trinity, it benefits us to listen to Him on how He said we should pray. His instructions give us a starting point for the conversation when we want to talk to God, and they give us a guide so our minds do not wander.

The goal of this book is to dissect Jesus' instructions to see the heart behind each section of the Lord's Prayer. With three contributing pastors, you will get insight into what each part of the Lord's Prayer means, as well as how to use it to enhance your own prayer life.

Pray is our lifeline, so learning about it is one of the most important things we can do. Whether you have never talked to God before in a deep way and want to learn, or if you are a long-time Christian but know you could be doing more in your prayers, this book will help you look closely at Jesus' words to pray the way that He prayed.

This step-by-step look at the Lord's Prayer started as a sermon series and has been adapted to a book that you can use over and over again and in group study.

It is intended to deepen your prayers, which will deepen your relationship with God, your Creator. Prayer gives you joy in the good times, strength and courage in the bad times, and helps you know who God is in a true relationship with Him.

PRAY LIKE THIS

I read a news article recently in the *Wall Street Journal* called "The Science of Prayer", and it said something interesting. The tone and purpose of the article acknowledged the fact that because of the COVID pandemic and everything that has gone with that, people are asking deep questions and praying more than they used to.

Here is a quote from Amy Wachholtz, Associate Professor and Clinical Health Psychology Director at the University of Colorado in Denver: "Imagine carrying a backpack hour after hour. It will start to feel impossibly heavy. But if you can hand it off to someone else to hold for a while, it will feel lighter when you pick it up again. This is what prayer can do. It lets you put down your burden mentally for a bit and rest."[1]

If we are honest with ourselves, each of us is carrying a heavy burden. Maybe it is a burden of fear and anxiety related to illness. Maybe it is frustration and righteous anger over the sin of racism. Maybe it is pressure you are dealing with at work, in your marriage, or in your relationships.

Whatever it may be, if we are honest, all of us have a burden we are carrying, and certainly there is an element of truth to what this professor wrote. When we look at Scripture in Matthew 11:28-30, Jesus even says:

Come to me all you who labor and are heavy laden, and I will give you rest. Take my yoke upon you, and learn from me, for I am gentle and lowly in heart, and you will find rest for your souls. For my yoke is easy and my burden is light.

Certainly, our burdens are heavy, and we want to unload them. Prayer is a component that lets us lay our burdens down at Jesus' feet and leave them there. That is good and biblical. But, if you pay attention to the quote and the context of the article, it is really painting a very self-serving view of prayer.

Scripture, on the other hand, teaches us so much more than that about what prayer is. I invite you to journey with me as we study how to pray like Jesus prayed.

Why Study The Lord's Prayer?

Now, you may ask, "Why do I need to even study the Lord's Prayer?" Well, there are many reasons, and I will present three to you. First, we are walking in a relationship, and in any relationship, communication is key.

You can compare that to the marriage relationship, a working relationship, or a parenting relationship. Prayer is a communication tool that we have to cultivate our relationship with God, and there is an element where discipline is a part of a healthy habit of praying regularly.

For a practical matter of application, consider the impact on family dynamics when the members of the household actually talk. Basic communication is essential for being known and for knowing others. Even more so, when we consider our relationship with God, the privilege of communication is a gift.

Hebrews 1:1-4 reminds us that God is speaking and has spoken for generations. Each day He speaks through the person of Jesus and draws us deeper into relationship with Himself.

Second, prayer causes us, as individuals, as a church, as a community, a culture, a nation and world to be awakened to new life. In fact, that was the whole purpose of that *Wall Street Journal* article. It was an awakening to more, to seeking answers to some really deep, intentional questions.

This is a natural response for humanity when we face crises and trials. When we go through something, we cry out to God as the supreme authority of the world. We cry out to Him in desperation, because we know we cannot do this without Him.

For many they feel distant and disconnected, while also possessing a deep desire for more. God desires to speak to you and reveal Himself to you. The answers you seek are known in Him, and can be found in pursuit of Him through prayer.

Third, out of a desire for renewal, awakening, and revival, we want to listen to the Holy Spirit. The best way to listen is in prayer, and often, the Holy Spirit will guide us when we do not know where to turn or give new life to our spirits through prayer.

On the Lord's Prayer, specifically, Martin Luther said this: "In a word, the Lord's Prayer is the greatest martyr on earth. Everybody tortures and abuses it; few take comfort and joy in its proper use."[2]

What we desire during the course of this book is to lean in and learn to use the Lord's Prayer properly. Let's look at what God's Word has to say about prayer, in general, as we set the stage.

Pretending to Pray

We see in Matthew 6:5 a warning of sorts. It says:

And when you pray, you must not be like the hypocrites. For they love to stand and pray in the synagogues and at the street corners that they may be seen by others. Truly I say to you, they have received their reward.

Verse five begins with an assumption. Keep in mind this is to a largely Jewish audience. Jesus says, "When you pray..." This presupposes, like any good Jew would do, they are going to pray at three specific hours of the day: morning, afternoon, and evening. So He is saying, "Hey, when you are going through your normal routine of prayer, be warned about these things."

As we apply this in our context today, we do not practice that Jewish tradition, necessarily, of praying at three designated hours of the day. When *you* pray, it may be in your morning prayers. It may be in addition to praying with your family at night. Whenever your normal prayers are, heed this warning.

At first pass, when you glimpse over this for the first time, it seems to suggest that public prayer is wrong. But we are actually going to see that it is communicating something different. We must first recognize that faith and prayer are not a game. Church is not a game. Church is not a social club only to gain community status. Prayer and faith are deliberately woven into the DNA of our spirit, the way that God has created us to be in relationship with Him.

In fact, specifically, as we read the intent of this verse, public prayer is very appropriate when it is practiced with the right motives. A public prayer should really represent the overflow of a vibrant personal prayer life.

The warning here is specifically written to not be like the hypocrites. In the Greek language, the word *hypocrite* means an actor or a pretender. So the prayer of a hypocrite is not true prayer; it is only acting. It goes no deeper than the lips. Men may hear it, but it does not reach to the ear of God.

What is more, prayer ought not to be for the purpose of gaining status and praise or just be a summary of a sermon. Instead, it should reflect a genuine conversation with God.

Sometimes, perhaps people use prayer as an escape. "I just want to get away." And sometimes we *should* get away and be alone. In fact, Jesus did that. But we must be careful not to fall into the trap of thinking that prayer and real life do not intersect with each other. The danger of that is a slippery slope toward a dualistic way of life, which means one's faith life and public life are two separate things.

God wants to consume all of us.

The intent of the command here that we read in Matthew 6:5 is not simply to prescribe certain places for prayer or to forbid praying in church. There is no condemnation of public worship or public prayer. Certainly, the early church even practiced corporate prayers in public. Their interpretation was: "It is not the place that harms, but the nature and the purpose."

We need to be careful that when we pray, we do not approach it with the posture of an actor or a hypocrite and one that just simply draws attention to himself rather than exercising submission to God as the supreme authority of the world.

So, what is the main point of verse five? It is that prayer (no matter the place) uttered with the intent of enhancing one's reputation or addressed not so much to God as to those looking on, is dangerous.

Dependency of Prayer

That leads us to a place of understanding the reference point, or the starting point, of prayer. Let's read Matthew 6:6:

But when you pray, go into your room and shut the door and pray to your Father who is in secret, and your Father who sees in secret will reward you.

Your attitude toward prayer is influenced by your view of God. I love Disney movies. In fact, one of my favorite Disney movies is *Aladdin*, and particularly (I know that this is debatable among some) I love the Will Smith version[3]. I thought it was fantastic! This young boy who is poor connects with a genie. The rules are: "If you rub the lamp, you get three wishes. You ask whatever you want, and you get it. But here are the things that you can ask for, and these are the things that you cannot ask for..."

Well, that is not how prayer works. You may not view God as a genie in the bottle, but you may view your relationship with God as having rules attached to it. Or maybe you *do* view God like a genie in the bottle, and all you do is ask Him to grant you your wishes.

What I want you to understand in the dependency of prayer is that our attitude toward prayer is influenced by our view of who God is. Many, or even most, view prayer as a ritual or routine that just helps us center and feel better about who we are.

For example, in this same article that I mentioned in *The Wall Street Journal,* a psychologist and Director of Social Psychology of Religion Lab at the Indiana University South Bend said, "Prayer can also foster a sense of connection with a higher power, your environment and other people, including the generations of people who have prayed before you."

Prayer does require discipline and routine, certainly, and one can turn a good thing into a ritual. But the power of prayer is understanding that it is not about me centering and connecting with *me*. It is about you connecting and understanding that a loving Creator, the Creator God and sustainer of the universe, desires to spend time with you and communicate with you.

I cannot walk with God in the cool of the Garden of Eden like Adam and Eve did every day, but I can walk and talk with God every day in a personal relationship with Him and in every moment of prayer. It is not about me centering myself or connecting with my feelings inside; it is about me communing with the Creator of the world.

Israel as a nation always historically viewed prayer as a conversation with a personal God. Let me give you some Old Testament examples. In Genesis 28, the God who spoke to Jacob in a dream revealed Himself this way: "I am the Lord, the God of Abraham your father and the God of Isaac." Again in Exodus 3:6 to Moses, God introduces Himself as the God of your father, the God of Abraham, the God of Isaac, and the God of Jacob.

It was in Exodus 3:14 that in this intimate conversation filled with power and reverence, He communicated to Moses His personal name of I Am. And because of this covenant commitment, He made Himself accessible to the people.

But that does not mean He becomes a magic genie in a bottle, ready to grant wishes with the snap of a human finger and the utterance of prayer. He responds to the prayers of the obedient and righteous in Proverbs 15:29. He despises superficial prayer in Isaiah 29:13. And He rejects the sacrifice of the wicked, we read in Proverbs 15:8.

In Matthew 6:6, there is an interesting phrase that offers a glimpse into the nature of God. It describes this as a God who sees in secret. Now, I have had some friends who use this verse out of context and inappropriately to suggest that we as Christians should keep our faith in a closet and not be public and vocal about it. I disagree. I want to shout from the rooftops that He is the King of kings and the Lord of lords. I do not want to hide in fear, but be vocal that He is the Savior, the Healer, and the Sustainer of the world.

Here we see a glimpse into His character because remember, my view of His character influences my attitude toward prayer. So, seeing here that He is a God who sees in secret suggests that the emphasis is on God's ability to see what takes place in the inner room, in the quiet moments, in our silent prayers, and in our thoughtful prayers.

The point is that prayer is not for us. It is not for me to center on me. It is not me just getting help with my problems like this burden that I am carrying. Nor is it for me to feel connected with others. It is about God, and it is for God. It requires no human audience. The soul in prayer must be turned only to God. The act of prayer, in and of itself, is a reminder of our dependence on God, the necessity of living through Him and for Him.

The act of prayer is a reminder of our dependence on God

All that being said, we still seem to make it so much harder than it really is. When asked to pray out loud, we often hesitate. Maybe you are in a life group, and someone asks you to pray. Maybe the family has gathered in a restaurant for dinner, and someone asks you to pray. These thoughts may go through your mind: *I can't pray. I don't know how to pray. I'm not good enough at it. That person is so much better with their words than I am. Let's let them pray.*

When we say and think those thoughts, it is as if we are im-plying that prayer is all about us, when in fact it is a matter of dependency on God and a desire to walk in relationship with Him.

The Simplicity of Prayer

Let's continue in verses seven and eight and talk about the simplicity of prayer:

And when you pray, do not heap up empty phrases as the gentiles do. For they think that they will be heard for their many words. Do not be like them, for your Father knows what you need before you ask him.

In verse five, there was this warning of not being like the hypocrite or the actor. Here in verse seven, there is this warning of not being like the gentile. Keep in mind this was written to a Jewish audience, and the gentiles represented this surrounding polytheistic culture. They viewed the world differently. They worshiped many gods, and each god had a specific purpose that they wanted to connect to.

When they needed fertility, they would pray to one god. When they needed rain, they would pray to another god. They would pray through chants and useless words and chatter.

I'll be honest; when I traveled to India, I got a glimpse of what this looks like. When you are truly immersed in a polythe-istic culture and seeing people interact and engage with other gods on a common basis, it really gets easier to understand this verse.

Here in Matthew 6:7, we see a comparison view of prayer with how the gentiles prayed. The magical prayer put one in touch with self, and they practiced incantations and mechanical repetition of a chant. This is "heaping up empty phrases."

This verb could mean meaningless words, or it could mean uttering senseless sounds or speaking incoherently or indistinctly. But this is not a biblical Christian view of prayer. More so, most Christians should know that prayer is much more than just bringing a grocery list of requests before God ("Do this; Do that").

We cannot treat prayer simply as using God as our genie in a bottle to get certain things done. There is one true living God. God is God, and we are His creation, walking in relationship with Him.

But there is also a concern here in the text that we might err on the opposite side. We might shy away from coming to God in prayer, because we do not want to disturb Him. We think, *He is too important, too awesome, too glorious to pay any attention to little old me.*

But verse eight calls for simplicity, directness, and sincerity in talking to God. The purpose of prayer is not just to exercise the tongue. It does not inform or remind God of anything; He already knows everything. Instead, it is an act of worship. It serves to cleanse the mind, purify the heart, and align the will of man with the will of God.

There is so much that we see in the world around us today that breaks our hearts: injustice, racism, the sins of others... Prayer aligns our will to the heart of God and leads us to repentance. Prayer is about God molding us and not us moving God.

Prayer is about God molding us, not us moving God.

Therefore, in light of all of that, learn to pray. In Matthew 6:9, Jesus is speaking, and He says, "Pray then like this. I have given you these warnings not to be like a hypocrite who is acting and not to be like a gentile who is using useless words. Instead, pray like this."

I don't know about you, but I really appreciate it when someone models the way for me. I enjoy it when someone shows me an example. I bet you do, too. In fact, how many times when you are trying to do that DIY project do you pull up YouTube, and somebody in the world has made a video showing you how to do that thing? We find value in that. We appreciate it.

We should not be threatened, intimidated or overwhelmed in the value or the importance of prayer to the point that we just choose not to do it because we do not know how. Jesus is saying, "I want to teach you." He gives the disciples (therefore you and me), a model of prayer. But it is not intended to be this ritual that you quote. It is a guide, and it provides a pattern.

The Lord's Prayer is easily divided into two sections. Over the next chapters, we are going to take one sentence or statement at a time. As we go through each one of them, you will see that they are truly landing in two buckets.

The first few phrases express the Kingdom of God and Kingdom values. They help place our focus properly on who God is. Then in the final few phrases, it expresses personal need and dependency on God. It somewhat follows the format that Jesus used when He summarized the entire known Scripture at one time in Matthew 22:37-40:

You shall love the Lord your God with all of your heart, with all of your soul, and with all of your mind. This is the great and first commandment. And the second is like unto it, you shall love your neighbor as yourself. And on these two Commandments depend all the law and the prophets.

Jesus told them that this is *how* they should pray, not necessarily *what* they should pray. The Lord's Prayer is a model, not a mantra. It is an example, a format, a formula. It is not magic words that we *have* to pray.

The Lord's Prayer is a model, not a mantra.

This is a discipline to learn, and it should take time to cultivate. If you are intimidated with the idea of prayer, you will get to learn how to pray. If you struggle through your prayer life, join the club. But do not use that as an excuse to not engage. Let's walk through this together, learning to pray like Jesus.

If it makes you feel any better, the disciples heard Jesus give them a model of prayer in Matthew 6, but they had to learn it again. The Lord's Prayer is written again in Luke 11, which describes a different point in time. It is about two years later that the disciples come to Jesus and say, "Jesus, will you teach us how to pray?" And Jesus says, "Okay, let me repeat for you word for word what I told you two years ago that you didn't understand.'"

The disciples needed this repeated lesson, and Jesus was patient with them. So, for you and me, regardless of how long we have been in relationship with Jesus, He is patient with us. He is drawing us closer in relationship with Him.

As we begin our study, right now, wherever you are, read the prayer out loud.

Our Father who is in heaven,
hallowed be your name.
Your kingdom come,
your will be done,
on earth as it is in heaven.
Give us this day our daily bread,
and forgive us our debts,
as we also have forgiven our debtors.
And lead us not into temptation,
but deliver us from evil.'
For Yours is the kingdom,
the power and the glory,
for ever and ever.
Amen.

DISCUSSION

1. Read Matthew 11:28-30. Are you carrying a burden in life alone? How can God help you?

2. Does it really make a difference if our prayers are ritualistic and recited? What role does prayer play in developing a personal relationship with God?

3. Read Matthew 6:5-8. Discuss why we hesitate to pray out loud in front of other people. How can we overcome this fear with a healthy understanding of prayer?

4. How do you typically start each prayer? Why does it make a difference?

5. Why is it important that we slow down and think about the words we say in prayer?

6. Why does it matter how we use God's name?

OUR FATHER

Imagine you are in a management position sitting at your desk or cubicle, and a team member bursts into your office. You can see the expression of stress on his face. He immediately jumps into telling you all of his problems, and he needs you to fix them.

You *should* be concerned. But there is a part of you that would love to just say, "Timeout. Hello. How are you today? At least acknowledge that I'm a human being before we just jump into the problem."

Or maybe it is your children. You are peacefully sitting on the couch sipping that cup of coffee, enjoying easing into the day, and a kid bursts into the room and immediately begins to tell you how his or her sibling took a toy. You're like, "Whoa, time out! Good morning. How are you?"

I don't know if you have that same frustration. I realize there are moments, crises, and emergencies, and we have to get right to business sometimes. But there is at some level a need to acknowledge that there are two human beings with needs, emotions, and desires connecting relationally before we just jump into asking for stuff.

It makes me wonder how God feels about our interactions with Him. I mean, just evaluate the majority of what our prayers feel like. "Hey God, help me. Hey God, give me this. Hey God, what in the world are you thinking?" We immediately just jump right in to asking for or complaining about something. I am not saying we sound like toddlers, but maybe sometimes we do.

As we walk statement by statement, verse by verse through the Lord's Prayer, we will see that there is a healthy way to begin a prayer in recognition of God's position name. Matthew 6:9 says:

Our Father in Heaven, hallowed be your name.

We Are Family

Another translation words it this way: "Our Father who is in Heaven, let your name be treated with reverence." The first point is this: We are family. We see this in the first word of the Lord's Prayer in "OUR". We are family. (You may have just started singing that song in your head).

We are family because we are on mission together. We are family because we have been forged through fire together. We are family because we share a common belief, and we have the same daddy. Note that it is not simply "*my* father," but it is "*our* father." That is a unifying, forging statement, and it is too powerful of a word just to gloss over in our desire to get to the good stuff of asking for forgiveness, asking for food, or asking for our needs to be met.

That little word *our* is full of meaning. It tells us that we are one in Christ Jesus. We are equal in the sight of God. Therefore, there should be no envy, no strife, and no parting spirit in our hearts, least of all in the hour of prayer. We need to sense and understand that we as believers are one in Christ.

What we will see is, so much of the Lord's Prayer contains plural statements. "*Our* debts, *our* bread, leading *us* into temptation." What we need to be reminded of is, since the Garden of Eden, since the creation of man, Adam and Eve in the garden, God has never intended man to be alone. We need relationships. That is one of the reasons why the COVID lockdown was so difficult. We need touch, presence, and connection. The forced distancing makes it so lonely.

A Really Good Place to Start

Second, our Father is in Heaven. This is a really good place to start. Let me tell you why. I don't know if you are a superhero/comic, DC/Marvel movie person, but don't you sometimes wish that you could be like Quicksilver or Flash? These guys move so fast that the world around them appears to be in slow motion. I think if I could choose my superpowers, this would be one of them. Either this or being able to teleport from one place to another. Those would be awesome.

But imagine if we could view the world around us in slow motion. Maybe for you, Marvel is a little too new of a reference.

Maybe we need to go back to *The Matrix* [4]. I want you to get that imagery as we talk about this place to start our prayers because the world moves at such a rapid pace that we often miss so much.

We should begin our prayers in slow motion. How do you commonly begin your prayer? It probably sounds something like this: "Dear Father," or, "Father God," or, "Hey, God." "Gracious Heavenly Father." "Good morning, Lord." Those are just sample ways that we commonly start a prayer, and none of them are wrong. In fact, all of them are rooted in a modern way of rephrasing "Our Father who is in Heaven."

Beginning your prayer that way is an attempt to model the prayer of Jesus. But often, we start our prayers with such a rushed pace, and we do not even slow down to acknowledge the words that just came out of our mouths. There is such weight, significance, and importance for us to breathe and have slow, *Flash* or *Matrix* moments.

Notice that Jesus' prayer does not begin with "our God" or "our Lord" (although both of those would be appropriate). It does not begin with "our King" (although he is going to immediately begin to speak of the Kingdom). Instead, He starts with "our Father." Why?

The character of our prayer depends upon our concept of God. The nature of your prayer is impacted by how you view God's character. It changes and influences the way you approach everything else.

The character of our prayer depends on our concept of God.

The Father Cares

To help us build a healthy concept of God on which we can build a healthy character of prayer, let's spend a few minutes unpacking what this might mean that God is our Father. Here is the first thing: The Father cares.

Dads play a critical role in the health of a family, the strength of a society, and the stability of humanity. And sadly in our culture, especially in American culture, we often find ourselves looking for a few good men. More than 33% of Americans live in a home without the physical presence of a father, and millions more live in a home where the father may be physically present but emotionally detached and distanced.

In fact, if this were classified as a disease, fatherlessness would be an epidemic worthy of a national emergency. I say that to say that if you, in your life presently or in the past, do not have a solid example of a father to contextualize a sound understanding of God as your father, I'm sorry. I hate that for you, and my prayer is that you will be able to push past and through that to discover peace in a relationship with a Father God who loves you, who can heal you from your hurt, and who will never leave you.

Instead, let's choose to focus on what should be the ideal. A dad should instinctively fulfill the role of provider and protector because he cares. Typically, he is thinking ahead and anticipating needs before they come. God even demonstrates this in Scripture in Matthew 6:8 -- "Your Father knows what you need before you ask him."

Matthew 6:26 says, "Look at the birds of the air. They neither sow nor reap nor gather into barns, and yet your heavenly Father feeds them. Are you not more valuable than they?" The God of the universe was not surprised by COVID-19, and for the many that suffered and are suffering still physically, emotionally, and financially, He is not surprised; He is not shocked. He is in control. Even when you doubt Him, and even when your situation seems overwhelming, the Father cares.

The Father is Close

Second, the Father is close. I do not know what your family has been like, but out of the pandemic, I have heard many stories of families spending an unusual amount of quality time together. Board games were reimagined. Family meals were rediscovered. People were fishing again. And that is really good.

In fact, I would say that it should not stop, because a close family is a godly family. It might mean that you need to create for your family some guardrails and barriers to say, "We are not going to get swept back up into the insanity rat race anymore. We are going to draw some lines in the sand now that we have tasted the goodness of what can be to make sure that we maintain some of these priorities for us as a family."

This idea helps us also understand the relationship between us and God as our Father. Beginning with the prayer that acknowledges God as my Father demonstrates the value of relationship. The Greek word for father is *patēr,* and translated into Aramaic, the word father is *abba.* It literally means daddy. It is an intimate term.

You see, "father" implies biology, but "daddy" implies intimacy, connection and closeness. What we need to understand is that a relationship to God as our daddy has been the design from the beginning. God created you to be in relationship with Him. This is the starting point of the whole Gospel story. Yes, we may want to communicate the Gospel, and we have been programmed over time with the "ABC" formula. A= admit to God that you are a sinner. B= believing that Jesus is Christ your Lord, and C= confess.

All of those are true and good, but that is actually not where it starts. It starts in the Garden of Eden. It starts in Genesis 2. It starts with God desiring a relationship. And because that relationship was broken from sin in the garden, that is what motivated God to send Jesus on this great rescue mission to reconcile us to Him. That is why, as we live out the Gospel, He has given to us the ministry of reconciliation as we model and demonstrate the Gospel.

Jesus attests to this close relationship between Him and God the Father. We see it in Mark 14:36. In his most stressful situation apart from the cross, He is in the Garden of Gethsemane. He is so stressed, blood is dripping down from His face, and He cries out, "Abba Father [in other words, Daddy], for you, all things are possible. Remove this cup from me. Yet not what I want, but what you want."

And that idea of viewing God as a daddy is not exclusive to Jesus. He desires it for us, as well. Galatians 4:6 tells us, "And because you are sons, God has sent the spirit of His Son into our hearts crying Abba Father," crying, "Daddy." Romans 8:15: "For you to not receive the spirit of slavery to fall back into fear. But you have received the spirit of adoptions as sons by whom we cry, ' Abba Father.'" or Daddy.

The relationship is unique between us and God. It is also shared among our faith family. We have the Father who cares and is close.

The Father Calls

Third, the Father calls. I have been blessed to have a great relationship with my father, my daddy, for years. Even to this day, if he calls my cell phone, and I don't answer, he will leave a voicemail, and without fail, it always goes like this: "Hey Son, this is your dad..." and he will go on to the message.

In my mind, I am thinking, "Did you have to identify yourself? When you call, I know who you are. One, you have whipped my butt. Two, I have heard you call my name when I was in trouble. Three, we have a good relationship. I know you."

God's voice is a recognizable voice, and regardless of your earthly example, I need you to know that we have a Father in Heaven who loves us. He cares for us. He calls us into a relationship, and we can call on Him through prayer. He is not just any daddy.

The phrase, "Father in Heaven," separates him from any earthly father, and it also preserves this distance of respect and relationship. It is one thing for me to have a close, intimate relationship with my dad. But it is another thing if I get so close that

I forget he is my dad, right? I cannot tell you the number of times I had to hear, "Listen here, Boy. I don't care how old you are; I will still turn you over my knee."

While the term *father* indicates intimacy, the addition of the parenthetical "in Heaven" speaks of his transcendence. The Father who cares for his children is enthroned in the heavens. It means he has the power to act on our behalf, and the hope of Heaven is secure because of His authority and conquering of death in the grave. He is beyond space and time, limitless, all powerful, slow to anger, and abounding in love.

You and I live in this social media-saturated world that leads us to be impatient. We want information now, and we think of things in fractions and milliseconds of time versus allowing sustained attention to really big ideas or deep conversations. And we cannot have prolonged silence.

We obsess over certainty, and in that, we may miss the God of Scripture, the Creator of the world who can be capable of coming and going, judging and forgiving, speaking and remaining silent. "In Heaven" implies that God is not simply Father for you, but He is Father for all the world. His love and care have extended through all the earth.

This challenge, then, is for us to pray to our Father who is in Heaven, showing that I have equal access to the Father no matter where I am. No matter where you are, no matter how far you have run, He cares. He is close. He calls your name, and you can call on Him. When it comes to prayer, we need to remember that how you start shapes how you finish.

How you start shapes how you finish.

When we get deeper into the Lord's Prayer, we are going to talk about petitioning for forgiveness, having our needs met, and relationships with other people. But how you start shapes how you finish.

Someday You'll Call My Name

He may be calling you into a relationship right now, and you may realize, *Man! I didn't even know that I could have a personal, intimate relationship with the Creator of the world!* He sent Jesus to this earth, so you can have that relationship, know Him as your daddy, and know that you are never alone. Whether it is now or later, it is as if He is saying, "Someday, you are going to call my name."

Now to the third section of this verse, "Our Father in Heaven, hallowed be your name." Now, I realize that word *hallowed* is not really a word that we toss around much. In fact, when you hear it, your mind may have immediately jumped to October 31st and costumes and candy.

That is not what we are talking about at all. Actually, this word is a really important word that means holy or reverent. Let's just be honest; our modern culture is void of a lot of pomp and circumstance. We do not have much in our world that has sacredness and rituals attached like we once had.

No analogy is perfect, but this is a close one. If you have never been, at some point in your life, you need to go to the Tomb of the Unknown Soldier in Arlington Cemetery and watch the changing of the guard ceremony. It is a place that is treated with reverence.

Everybody there is standing in silence, giving honor to that moment. Now, I realize that this pales in comparison to talking about the transcending Creator of the world, but it is an image of this attitude of treating something as very, very special.

It really begs the question, how do you treat holy things? Very, very carefully. That's how.

Imagine you are sitting across a table with a grandmother, and there has a fragile heirloom ceramic piece that has been passed down from generation to generation. She says, "I want to give this to you. It has been in my family for four generations. This is very special."

She tells you this great backstory to it and puts it in your hands. How would you handle that? You would not just drop it in your bag, right? I mean, you can imagine the sweat coming off of your brows as you try to walk with this thing because it has been entrusted to you, and you have got to treat it very carefully.

Again, it pales in comparison. There is no analogy that significant, but what we are trying to communicate here is, God has a name that is revered above all. It is holy and should be treated carefully. It should not just be flippantly tossed around.

The idea of a name does not just refer to what I call someone. It refers to that person and his or her character. It refers to his or her authority. So, when I speak of the name of God, I am speaking of all that God stands for. It should be treated as holy and honored because of His utter perfection and goodness.

In fact, God has commanded us not to use His name in vain. For generations, the Jewish tradition and culture has gone through great lengths to be very careful in how they even write the name of God.

In conversation, they use another name, maybe Adonai, which means "my Lord", because they do not want to speak the name and treat it improperly or disrespectfully.

How Can We Keep God's Name Holy?

There is so much in Scripture that we can point to that reminds us of the holiness of God. Here are several references:

Leviticus 20:3
Leviticus 22:2
Leviticus 32:1
1 Chronicles 16:10
1 Chronicles 29:16
Psalms 30:4
Psalm 33:11

These are just reminders of the magnitude, weight, significance, and holiness of God's name. When we honor God the Father as holy, we also acknowledge what He considers holy.

So here is the question: How can we keep God's name holy? It is not a ceremony that we can go to like the unknown soldier.

It is not an heirloom that we can hold physically in our hands. So what are some ways that we can respect His name as holy?

Recognize it as Sacred

Here is one thing: Recognize it as being sacred. Simply recognize, acknowledge the fact that it is a unique and special name. We have got to begin there. Recognize that it is not just a name that we can casually use.

Trust Him

Second, put some trust in it. God has proven Himself faithful over and over again in the past. And He will continue to prove Himself faithful in the present and in the future. You can trust Him. When you call, He will answer. He may not always give you the answer you want, and He may not always give you the answer when you want it, but He is always there. He is always listening. He always responds, and He is always present.

Respect His Name

You might ask, "But what is the difference between recognizing it and respecting it? Aren't those the same?"

Recognizing would say, "Yeah, that is special." Respecting it means, "I allow it to impact my prayers, my life, and my language. I realize that it is more than just the name, but it encompasses all that He represents." I allow that to impact my decisions because I am an image bearer of God, and I am a name bearer of the King.

I will paint it this way. There have been more times than I can count in my life when I have taken a group of kids somewhere. We've gone on mission trips, to ball games, and to Six Flags. Every time, without exception, I always give this speech:

"Remember, here are the safety rules... Stay in groups of ___. Be back at ___ . Remember that as you conduct yourself today outside of the umbrella of an adult, you represent the name of Jesus and ___ organization..."

My actions are not just about defaming *my* name. My sin, my action, and my behavior have the risk of defaming the name of God. So therefore, I have to respect, recognize, and acknowledge the holiness of it.

Choose Him Over Idols

It should lead me to choose Him over idols. "Well Ricky, what in the world do idols have to do with respecting the name of Jesus?" Well, if I choose to follow or worship an idol, what am I saying about the jealous God whose name deserves to be praised? I am saying, "I don't need you. I don't respect you. I don't recognize you. Instead, I recognize this idol." Idolatry is about finding a god we can control a god that can serve our desires.

When we pray "holy be your name," we are confessing that we will not abuse the holiness of God by attempting to put a leash on Him and then drag Him to our own crusades.

Wait

Fifth, I can respect and honor the name of God as holy by waiting. This is a way of showing respect. Let's go back to parenting. How many times, Dads, do we see our kid come in, and our immediate response is, "What do you want? How much is this going to cost me?"

Sometimes our kids ask us something, and we could immediately answer, but sometimes we intentionally make them wait. Why? Because it is good for them. Sometimes it is good for them to wait, because in that waiting, it is a way of showing respect to our authority.

"I'll give you the answer when it is time for you to have it. In the meantime, you just need to wait."
"Why?"
"Because I said so."

As a kid, you hated that answer, but there are some times when that is the right answer. "Because I said so." There should be no other discussion.

There are some times that God will make a demand, set an expectation, or call us out for something, and we may question God. It is as if He is simply saying, "Because I said so. That is why you need to do it that way. I am God. I brought you into this world, and I can sure enough take you out."

To keep God's name holy entails waiting on Him, waiting in prayer, and waiting in obedience. Waiting is perhaps the hardest thing for people to do. We are reminded of our need to have a slow-motion moment. Take a deep breath, and slow down. You may still feel the need to rush into your manager's office and unload on him or her. You may still have a kid come into the living room and unload on you, making demands. Those things may still happen, and they may be outside of your control.

But what we can control is to be more intentional in our prayers with a deeper acknowledgement of who we are talking to. Let's choose to slow down when we start our prayers. It is that starting point of recognizing our Father and the intimacy He deserves to have as our daddy. Respect His authority and power, and honor the holiness of His name.

It is in His nature to call, to care, and to love. And it should impact our thoughts, our lives, our behaviors, and our prayers. So as we pray through the Lord's Prayer, let's slow down. Let's breathe it in, and wait. Read this prayer out loud again, like we did in the first chapter.

Our Father who is in heaven,
hallowed be your name.
Your kingdom come,
your will be done,
on earth as it is in heaven.
Give us this day our daily bread,
and forgive us our debts,
as we also have forgiven our debtors.
And lead us not into temptation,
but deliver us from evil.'
For Yours is the kingdom,
the power and the glory,
for ever and ever.
Amen.

DISCUSSION

1. How does your view of God and His character impact your prayer life?

2. How has idolatry crept into American culture, and how can that impact your prayer life?

3. What is the difference between God as our Father and God as our Daddy?

4. Share a story of when parents made a hard decision that was best for the family. How does this model God's love for us?

5. Read Matthew 6:10, and discuss why it is hard to give up control of our lives. Why is it important to submit to God's plan?

6. If the world says, "Do what makes you happy," but God desires us to please Him, how do we live in this tension?

THE HARDEST PRAYER TO PRAY

Matthew 6:10

Your kingdom come, your will be done, on earth as it is in heaven.

Did you know that the disciples did not ask Jesus to teach them how to preach? They did not even ask Jesus to teach them how to sing. They asked Jesus, "Would you please teach us how to pray?" In other words, there is a right way to pray, and there is a wrong way. That is why we need to be taught by the Lord.

Do you know what the shortest prayer in the Bible is? How about the longest? The prayer of Jesus in John 17 can be read in five minutes. The prayer of Solomon and the dedication of the Temple can be read in six minutes. The prayer of Nehemiah is the longest prayer in the Bible (Nehemiah 9:5-38). The prayer of Peter, I believe, is the shortest prayer, which says, "Lord, save me (Matthew 14:30)".

But what is the most *difficult* prayer in the Bible? I believe it is this one in Matthew 6:10: "Your will be done."

What is God's will? God's will is what He says He will do, and His will is that we do what He tells us to do.

God's Word and God's Spirit cannot be opposed to one another. God telling us what to do is the will of God. For religious people of Jesus' day, the concept of God's fatherhood was hard to grasp. They were used to the word *Lord*. They were used to the word *King*. They were used to the word *Judge*.

But they did not understand and could not even fathom the idea that He is our Father. The Old Testament spoke maybe less than half a dozen times about God as the Father. But in the New Testament, it mentions it more.

People often ask me, "How do I know the will of God?" Have you asked that question? I hope it will be answered by the time you finish this chapter.

Some Christians I know who are great theologians always come to me wanting to study Matthew 24 and Daniel 9. They want to understand portions of the Bible that they do not understand.

Let me help you with that. To understand what you *do not* understand, first obey what you *do* understand. To understand the will of God, first obey what you do understand about His will, and whatever He tells you to do is His will.

I am reminded of a little boy who prayed this prayer and asked, "A Father who is in Heaven? How does He know my name?" God loves *all* of us. But God also loves *each* of us.

We can know the will of God, and we can know the leadership of God. But before we talk about what it is to pray, "Your will be done," I want to mention some false things about praying that.

One of the false concepts people have is thinking the will of God is a detailed roadmap for your life. False. Praying in the will of God is not the roadmap of your life. Rather, it is a *relationship* with your Heavenly Father.

Second, the will of God is designed to make your lifestyle miserable. False. It is to make your life magnificent and filled with love, joy, peace, and His presence.

Third, the will of God can be known only by a certain group of people (like pastors, missionaries, or theologians). False. God has a plan for everyone, even the wicked, evil individual.

Fourth, the will of God is difficult to discover; God hides His will. False. The secret things belong to the Lord, our God. But the things that are revealed belong to us and to our children forever.

The reality is that we do not find the will of God; the will of God finds us.

Here is the problem: When we ask God's will to be done in us, we are asking that our will be overturned, if necessary. Another problem is, when we ask for the will of God to be done on earth as it is in Heaven, this must be a reference to angelic beings in Heaven. Psalms 103:20 says:

Bless the Lord, oh you His angels, you mighty ones who do His Word, obeying the voice of His Word.

Did you know that the enemy of God's will is often our will? Do we want Jesus, or do we want what Jesus can give? The will of God is Jesus Himself.

When we talk about Heaven, God's will is always done. It is done instantaneously, completely, and joyfully in Heaven. It is done without any hesitation or question. But God's will is rarely done on earth willingly.

After all, there are 7 billion people living on this earth, and there are 7 billion wills. There is only one will in Heaven. Are you interested in doing the will of God today? How often do we sincerely pray, "Your will be done"? It almost seems like a hopeless prayer request, doesn't it? Here are four reasons why.

Relinquishing the Rights of Your Will to Another

Number one, to pray "your will be done" means you are relinquishing the rights of your will to another.

In other words, you must be submissive to God. Only one will can be done at a time: either yours or God's. The Apostle Paul is a perfect example of how we should respond to God. We see when he was saved on the way to Damascus, he asked God two things: "Who are you, Lord?" and, "What is it that you want me to do?"

The rest of his life was consumed by doing the will of God. Ephesians 5:17 says, "Therefore, do not be foolish, but understand what the will of the Lord is."

It can be understood and obeyed. Believers, listening to God comes with consequences. If I tell my boys to do something, and they do not do it, it is not that they didn't understand my will; they just didn't want to do it.

God's will is so clear. It is written in His Word. We have got to obey what is written. Whatever He tells me, that is His will. Prayer is not asking God to do something that He is not willing to do. Prayer is asking God to enable you to do *exactly* what He tells you to do. Prayer is the heart of worship, and I believe some tears are liquid prayers.

Do Not Doubt That God Intends the Best for You

Reason number two: To pray "your will be done" means you do not doubt that God intends the best for you. In other words, when you pray "your will be done", you must have confidence in God. If you do not have the complete trust that God's will is best, you will never be able to pray sincerely, "Let your will be done." Our biggest question is not, is there a God? Most people believe there is. Our biggest question is, is there a God in Heaven who cares about me?

Even many Christians might answer that question with a, "No, He really doesn't care about me." Is God always there? Yes.

As long as you doubt God, that prayer will be impossible to pray.

Doing the will of God is not easy, Friend, but it is enjoyable. I love what David said in Psalms 40:8:

I delight to do your will, oh God.

Joy comes from knowing that God gives you the grace to accomplish the purpose for which He called you.

It Involves Suffering and Pain

Number three: to pray "your will be done" means that it involves suffering and pain. Therefore, you must be strengthened by God. The will of God cannot take you where the power of God cannot keep you.

Jesus our Lord wrestled in prayer in the Garden of Gethsemane. His hour had finally come. A threatening cloud of darkness hovered over Him. All of the atrocities of human beings, the flood of their insolent iniquities, and the viciousness of their despicable depravity were all present in the cup.

He recoiled, and then He prayed, "Father, if thou be willing, remove this cup from me. Nevertheless, not mine, but thine be done."

This was so hard for Him to pray that the writer of Matthew, in chapter 26, mentioned it twice: in verses 39 and 42. Jesus asked the disciples, "Can you not watch with me?" Then the Bible says He went a little farther and prayed, "Remove this cup from me." Then He prayed again. These are not the words of unbelief; these are the words of faith.

They are the words of a man who understood fully what it would cost to do the will of God. John 6:38 says, "For I have come to do the work of Him who has sent me, not to do my own will." Lord Jesus is exhibit A of what it costs to pray "your will be done". It cost Him His life.

No wonder He struggled in Gethsemane. We struggle with it, too. Many Christians that I know in my personal life do not want to know the will of God. They really don't. They only want God to rubber stamp their will. For many Christians, it is like Christ is an architect. They do not want His design; they only want Him to redesign what they already have in their minds.

It Goes Against Everything This World Stands for

Finally, the fourth reason why praying "your will be done" is so hard is that it goes against everything the world stands for. You must be separated *to* God.

It almost seems that God has abandoned the world to satanic forces. But God is not sitting idly by. He is still in charge, and He is still accomplishing His eternal plans and purposes. I like what C.S. Lewis said. "There are two kinds of people in the world. Only two kinds. Those who say to God, 'Your will be done,' and those to whom God says in the end, 'Have it your way; your will be done.'" 5Which kind are you?

1 John 2:17 says, "And the world is passing away along with its desires. But whoever does the will of God abides forever." Don't fret. Ask God to guide you every day of your life. I love Psalms 86:11-13:

Teach me your way, oh God, that I may walk in your truth. Unite my heart to fear your name. I give thanks to you, oh Lord my God, with my whole heart, I will glorify your name forever. For great is your steadfast love towards me.

Many people ask me, "How do I know the will of God on whether He wants me to buy a pickup truck or a Sedan? How about a house in Columbus or a house by the beach?" Well, I do not have a verse for that, but I will tell you one thing. The steps of the man are established by the Lord when he delights in His ways (Psalms 37:23).

Do you want God's leading? Do you want God to show you His will? He will instruct you if you obey Him. But here is the warning from our Lord in Matthew 7:21-23:

Not everyone who says unto me, "Lord, Lord," will enter the Kingdom of Heaven. But the one who does the will of my Father, who is in Heaven.

What is the will of the Father? His will is in John 6:40, that "Everyone who looks on the Son and believes in Him should have eternal life. And I will raise him on the last day."

Will you pray today with a sincere heart, "Lord, let your will be done in my life"? Mary Brainard wrote a hymn in the late 1800's titled *I Know Not What Awaits Me*, which says:

I go on not knowing.
I would not if I might.
I'd rather walk in the dark with God
Than go alone in the light.
I'd rather walk by faith with Him
Than to go alone with sight.[6]

This is Samuel Thomas' (my) version of Matthew 6:10: "Lord, I cannot have it all, but you can have all of me. Let your will be done." As I said in the beginning, doing the will of God is not easy, but it is enjoyable.

In 2001, I was with my father in South India with a team from Liberty University. I will never forget, it was an evening crusade meeting. My dad wanted us to get plenty of chairs, because he knew that so many people would come. We rented 5,000 chairs!

The service was supposed to start at 6:00pm, and it started pouring. My dad said, "Son, why don't you pray that God stops this rain?" After I finished praying, it didn't stop raining. He looked at me, and he said, "Son, why don't you ask your friends from Liberty University if they would sing a couple of songs?"

The guy who was in charge looked at me and said, "Go and tell your father we have $200,000 worth of equipment. We have covered it under the plastic, and we don't want to take any chances. Why not ask him if we can come tomorrow?"

So of course, I had to be the carrier of that message. I went to my father and said, "Dad, they think we should do it tomorrow." He said, "Go and ask them, how much does it cost to give me one microphone?" So of course, I'm walking in that rain back to the musicians.

They said, "Okay, he can use a mic." I'll never forget, he put a napkin on his head, and he walked to the stage. Of course, in Indian culture, if your dad is walking in the rain, you do not sit in the car like a snob. You are supposed to stand outside. So I am standing outside, getting soaked, waiting for him to get to the platform.

He preached for 59 minutes! How many chairs did we have? 5,000 chairs. What was on those chairs? Raindrops. Not one chair was occupied. All the chairs were empty.

When he came back to the car, I, being a smart aleck, had to ask, "Do you feel satisfied? Do you feel happy?" He said, "Yeah Son, I know what I did. I did the will of God."

That was 2001.

In 2008, he had a heart attack and stroke while he was in the US. We finally took him to India for treatment, and he was taken to South India in Kerala. They put him in the hospital for about six months there.

The last day at the hospital, before he was shifted to his headquarters in Kota, North India, as we were leaving that day, my dad's younger brother, my dad's younger sister, and my two sisters were in the room. The nurse comes in and tells us, "There is an individual who wants to meet your father. Would you let him come in?"

I said, "Sure. He can come in." You have to understand Indian culture. As soon as he comes in, he touches my dad's feet, he kisses, and he cries. He was not idolizing my father, but that was just the respect he had for him. Dad could not speak; his right movement was paralyzed.

This man said, "Sir, you may not know me, but in 2001, when you were preaching in that rain, I was standing under a tree. You could not see me, but I was on my way to commit suicide, and I said to my friend, 'This is a crazy man preaching in the rain. Maybe he has something important to say. How about I just stay here and listen to him?'"

He said, "Sir, that rainy day, I gave my life to Christ. Ever since then, I was discipled by the local church, and then they paid my way to go to the Bible college. I am now pastoring a church with 175 believers."

Friends, one of the ways to know the will of God is to lead people to Christ. Let the lost come to know Him. "Not my will, but thine be done. Lord, I cannot have it all, but you can have all of me."

"Our Father who is in heaven,
hallowed be your name.
Your kingdom come,
your will be done,
on earth as it is in heaven.
Give us this day our daily bread,
and forgive us our debts,
as we also have forgiven our debtors.
And lead us not into temptation,
but deliver us from evil.'
For Yours is the kingdom,
the power and the glory,
for ever and ever.
Amen."

DISCUSSION

1. How do you typically respond when the will of God contradicts what culture says is appropriate? Discuss examples where we experience this tension each day.

2. Read Hebrews 13:20-21, and discuss how God has equipped you to do His will.

3. Read Luke 22:42, and discuss how Jesus submitted to God's will even when it meant He would face suffering. What can we learn from His example?

4. Share a story with the family of a time when you received an unexpected blessing during a time of need. How did that act remind you of God's awareness of your basic needs?

5. Read Matthew 6:11. What is this verse teaching you about being dependent on God, and would you say that God has been faithful to give you daily bread?

6. Read Matthew 7:7, and discuss how you handle the tension between being content with what you have and asking for more of something. Can you enjoy nice things and still find contentment in God?

OUR DAILY BREAD

I am going to make a couple of confessions. The first is a parenting confession. If you have kids, if you have ever babysat before, or if you have watched over a group of young children, you know that they have this amazing gift, or skill, of asking for stuff… nonstop.

It is as if they are always in need of something, yet are unsure of what exactly it is. However, they instinctively know to come to you for it. The first five or ten times in the morning, it's okay, right? It is the parent thing you expect. And in some small way, you actually enjoy it because it makes you feel needed and wanted.

We are going through this right now with our youngest son, Lewis. He just asks for stuff all the time (or really, makes demands). "I want this. I want that one. I want Mama. I want Daddy. I want Bubba. I want up. I want down. Play with me…"

Again, the first few times in the morning are okay. You embrace it, and you're like, *this is my parental calling.* Then by the 75th time before lunch, your nerves start to get frazzled a little bit. By the 200th time and by the end of the day, you are really starting to question, *are children, in fact, a gift from the Lord?*

It is fascinating to me how a young child never really has internal issues with asking mom or dad for something. They have no internal counter telling them, "This is the 20th time you have asked for this. You might want to wait a minute before you ask again."

Children demonstrate to us an incredibly important principle about our relationship with our heavenly Father. One of the greatest things about prayer is, we never have to worry that God is going to be bothered by our coming to Him. We never have to worry that it is going to be some sort of an inconvenience.

He is never too busy working on something else that we should wait a little while before we come in and ask something of Him. He loves for us to speak with Him and make requests. He longs for us to commune with Him, and He is not bothered at all by our asking.

In the Lord's Prayer, Jesus teaches us how to pray for ourselves. How do we pray for our needs? Let's read Matthew 6:11.

Give us this day our daily bread.

It may seem short and sweet, but there may be no greater proclamation of the Gospel in the Lord's Prayer than in these seven words right here. There is a shift in focus happening. Remember, the Lord's Prayer opens by focusing our minds on God and His priorities. The first three petitions of the Lord's Prayer are all about God's concern for His name to be hallowed, or exalted, as Father.

If the idea of God as Father bothers you because you had a bad experience with your earthly dad, can I give you some encouragement? God is not a reflection of our earthly fathers. He is the *perfection* of our earthly fathers. In every way that you feel that your earthly dad may have failed you or hurt you, be it spiritually, emotionally, or physically, God is not a reflection of that. He is the perfection of that.

He is the ultimate fulfiller and satisfaction of every little hole in your heart or in your life where you feel your earthly dad has let you down. That is why we can sing songs like "Good, Good Father" [7]. That is why we can read texts like "Our Father in Heaven".

The previous chapter was about the hardest prayer that a believer can pray: God's Kingdom come, and His will be done. In fact, of all of the petitions in the Lord's Prayer, only one has to do with a material blessing.

It could seem like this chapter's text is a bit selfish or a bit of turning the spotlight off of God and on to ourselves. But my hope is to lead you into an understanding that by coming to God and asking for our basic needs, that is one of the highest forms of worship from a child of God.

For you to unashamedly come before Him and say, "I cannot make it without you today. I am 100% dependent on you today, Lord," is profound worship. That is ultimate submission of self and the full exaltation of God.

I would like for us to study this sentence, "Give us this day our daily bread," one part at a time. There are three really important components to this prayer that I want you to draw from.

Give Us

Let's start with the first phrase, "give us". If you were reading this completely out of context, pulling it out of the book of Matthew and writing it on the index card, if you read it for the first time, it may appear or seem at first glance that this is abrupt or demanding.

It seems to be coming on a little strong, because there is no, "Excuse me," or, "Hey, when you have a minute, do you think you could…" There is none of that. It is just straight to the point. There might be a little rub inside of you if you think back to table manners.

But remember what the writer of Hebrews says in chapter four, verse 16:

Let us then with confidence, draw near to the throne of grace, that we may receive mercy and find grace to help in time of need.

This statement "give us" is not one of disrespect or irreverence. It is not one of selfish demand. It is actually one of confidence on behalf of the believer that God is able. We ask because we know that God is gracious and generous. Paul says in Ephesians 3:20:

To him who is able to do immeasurably more than all we ask or imagine, to him be the glory.

Here is the good news in that one verse: You cannot out-ask God. I think for many of us, we hold back on what we really, really want to pray, and we hold back on what we really want to ask for because there is a part of us that thinks, *Man! If I ask for this, it might be the one thing that depletes God of the rest of His resources.*

Okay, that can't happen. What this verse is telling us is, as soon as you feel like you may be asking too much or requesting too much, remember that He can do immeasurably more than that and more than what you can imagine (Ephesians 3:20). You cannot even think of a scenario that would be asking too much of God. That is comforting for us that we should be able to boldly approach Him and ask.

I want to draw special attention specifically to that word, *us.* In chapter one, we talked about the familial nature of this prayer, specifically pointing to *our* Father. That same tone carries here and throughout this entire Lord's Prayer.

What I mean by that is, there are not two versions of this prayer. There is not one that you pray when you are by yourself, just praying for you and then another version that you pray when you are in a group or in a church setting. No, when we pray to God, *our Father*, we speak words of community: our Father, our bread, our sins, those who sinned against us, and deliver us.

The reminder is that you are a part of a much, much larger family, one that is filled with different skin colors, different languages, and different tastes in things. We all have different quirks (and I certainly have my own), but we all have the same heavenly Father. *Give us* is both personal and corporate.

Let's go through a couple of verses together to understand that a little better. Paul says in Philippians 2:4: "Let each of you look not only to his own interests, but also to the interests of others." That's *us*. In Galatians 6:2, he says, "Bear one another's burdens." In 1 Corinthians 10:24, Paul said, "Let no one seek his own good, but to the good of his neighbor." *Us* is always you plus at least one other. That is how it works.

As you pray, "Give us," maybe think about your coworker or a teacher. Maybe think about the single mom who lives in your neighborhood and is struggling to make ends meet right now or that teenager who is just in a really dark place because he is struggling with the loss of his mom or dad. Maybe think about someone you know who is sick or ill.

By praying, "Give us," and believing those are not just words, but you actually believe what you are saying, you are saying that you trust God to provide abundantly enough for you to be sacrificially generous to others. What you are really saying is, "God, I have full faith and trust that you can provide for me and my family. We will be filled and full, and we will be perfectly fine. I will be able to give to others not my scraps and leftovers, but sacrificially generously.

When we start praying things like, "Give us," and we pray that with boldness, belief, and faith, we know that God will give abundantly enough to me and to my family so that I can be more sacrificially generous.

This Day

What comes next in this verse as we unpack it phrase by phrase? *This day.* I want to be honest with you; here is confession number two: I probably struggle with this part the most, and here is why.

I am learning as a dad of two boys how fast groceries disappear from our house. It is like every other day, my wife says, "Hey Frank, I have another pickup order of food to go get." I don't understand why they disappear so quickly, and I know it only gets worse as they get older.

I may be the only one like this, but I have this tension inside to make groceries last. I'll tell my son, "I know we just got this little container of strawberries; we just can't eat all of them today. Let's set a goal to go three days with the strawberries."

I have this tension to make groceries last, and it is not because I have this memory in my childhood of being without food. That wasn't a part of my childhood. But I am a product of my dad's household. I do remember my dad setting forth some expectations.

"Hey Son, you can have a bowl of cereal, just not the whole box," or, "If you want to make a sandwich and you want to put cheese on it, that's fine. Just one slice of cheese, not three slices."

I once had a friend spend the night at our house when I was in school. The next morning, he got up and fixed himself a bowl of cereal. He ate at our house the way he eats at his house. He opened a fresh box of cereal and depleted the whole thing. I was panicked that I was going to get in trouble because, I mean, the expectation in our house was that the box of cereal would last more than one breakfast on a Saturday morning.

Here is the thing: Even though I have this tension to make groceries last, that is the exact *opposite* of what this verse in the Lord's Prayer is teaching us.

To pray, "Give us this day" means that you are looking in full dependence on God to give you every day all that you need to fulfill His will for that day. This is radical trust. This is where trust and worry collide.

Let's just be honest and own some things about today. There are a lot of questions we have right now about today. And there are even *more* questions about tomorrow that we do not have answers to.

My wife is a public school teacher. We are having a lot of conversations right now about what school is going to be like in the future. Are jobs secure? What is the social climate in our country going to be like weeks or months down the road?

For many, these questions are real, worth asking, and worth talking about. But also, these are questions that can cause a heightened sense of anxiety or stress, which is why this prayer for us is so important. God does not want you to worry about how you are going to survive tomorrow, next week, or next month. He just wants you to focus right now on living abundantly today.

When you pray, "This day," you are acknowledging that God gives abundant life one day at a time. Think about the Israelites as they wandered through the desert. God provided manna for them each day to feed them, right? But there was a catch. There was a little clause in the provision of, "Hey, I'm going to let it rain down manna from Heaven. You are going to be able to get your fill, but here is the catch: You can only get enough for today."

In fact, Exodus 16:21 tells us that when the sun grew hot, it melted. If you were trying to store up a whole bunch of manna to last for tomorrow or the next day, by midday, that stuff was gone. God was telling them, "I will provide everything you need, but only for today."

This teaches us a really important characteristic about God and speaks a lot of His character. He is an ever-present, all sufficient God for tomorrow, which means you can 100% trust that He is able to do for you tomorrow everything and then some that He did for you today.

Think about that. Why else would He let it rain food from Heaven and then also, in the same day, allow it to melt away? It was to demonstrate, "Hey, you can trust me."

Our oldest son, Austin, likes to ask a lot of "tomorrow" questions, and he tends to start that at about breakfast. He will sit at the table and ask, "So Dad, what are you going to do tomorrow?" or, "Dad, on Saturday, do you think we can go to the pond?" (This is on Tuesday.) I know it is probably innocent right now, but I do not want it to become a stumbling block for him later.

I like to just gently nudge him back to today, saying, "Hey Buddy, today is a great day. Let's just focus on today." Or, "Today is a gift. Let's just enjoy this gift today."

I appreciate his enthusiasm about tomorrow, and it is not to say that tomorrow doesn't have its concerns or that it is wrong to make plans in advance. But what I am trying to subtly teach Austin in nudging him back to today is this practice of contentment. Real contentment, I believe, leads to peace. Peace, we know, is rooted in our trust in the Lord.

Proverbs 3:5 tells us, "Trust in the Lord with all your heart." You and I were designed to operate on trust, but the corrosion element to trust is worry. Worry and trying to figure out how you are going to do things all on your own will corrode trust.

When we pray, "This day," we are practicing contentment. We are saying, "God, I am going to be satisfied and full with my condition today. I don't have to buy everything off the shelves today for fear that you won't be able to provide for me tomorrow."

That is good news for all of us. God is able and has promised, "Hey, I got you. I am going to provide."

Our Daily Bread

Now, what exactly are we asking for when we pray, "Give us this day"? What exactly are we wanting Him to give us? --Our daily bread.

Third confession: There have been many times when I have decided on where I am going to eat just solely based on the free bread that they give. There is just something about breadsticks or a freshly-baked loaf wrapped in a blanket, put in a basket with some butter on the side.

Or just think about the cheese biscuits at Red Lobster, because those things are *good*, and you only go there for those things, right? I think they serve other food, but you are there for the biscuits.

Bread is good for you, and it is a staple for life. Throughout the Bible, bread is pretty amazing. We know it is really important, because it is mentioned no less than 492 times from Genesis through Revelation.

It also carries with it a lot of meaning and symbolism. Just think through what it was like to wake up in the morning as an Israelite in Exodus 16 and actually see it raining food from Heaven. Allow your imagination to have some fun and just wake up, go outside of your little tent or hut. Breakfast is falling all around you. Imagine what that was like, that God fed his people for 40 years that way, by having it fall from the sky. Yes, it was critical to their survival, but what God was demonstrating to them was that everything we have is from Him.

For many people, the struggle of, "Where is my next meal going to come from?" is a real thing. But your daily bread also might be something different. It might be medication, a job, finances, or it may be just a solid grant to depend on in a time of uncertainty.

When we pray *daily bread*, we are reminded that God has already promised to provide, and He is faithful to deliver not just what you need physically, but also to satisfy your spiritual needs. John 6:35 tells us:

Jesus told them, I am the bread of life. Whoever comes to me will never become hungry. Whoever believes in me will never become thirsty.

Daily bread is all-encompassing. By Jesus's death, burial, and resurrection, He brings our soul to life and offers a way to salvation. That means that in Christ, the bread of life, we find forgiveness and freedom, two things that you cannot find, buy, or do on your own. That is good news for us!

It makes this Lord's Prayer a little more clear that everything in it actually points back to Jesus. If we were to read this verse the way it was originally written, the order would be very, very different. If we were to read this first as it is written in the Greek, we would actually say, "Bread, our daily, give us this day."

It is a bit Yoda-like, but in the Greek language, sentences were written with the most important words or phrases first. They wanted to draw your attention to what they wanted to emphasize. As Greek was being translated into English, the order was changed around just to make it easier to read and a little more clear to us.

But if we are not careful, we will miss the most important thing. In the English, the emphasis appears to be on *give us*, because again, if you just look at that one sentence all by itself, that is what your mind is drawn to. It seems to be pointing a lot to self. But in the original language, the emphasis is on *bread*, the thing that is given. -more importantly, the One who is giving it.

This prayer, the entirety of the Lord's Prayer, and then specifically verse 11, *Give us this day our daily bread* is not selfish at all. It is not like the constant begging of a child for something, because the focus is never actually on us in this verse. We are children of a heavenly Father, a loving and generous Father who just happens to own everything.

We do not have to hesitate to ask Him to provide for us. When you do that, when you have an honest moment in prayer, you are going to say, "Lord, I need you right now, and this is how I need you. This is what I need." When you actually have those honest, vulnerable moments, you are complimenting and praising Him. You are telling Him how loving, generous, and powerful you actually believe Him to be.

That is an act of worship, and it allows us to pray boldly and confidently. You might ask, "Frank, why do we pray anyway? What is our big motivation to pray? If God knows what we need, if He is a good Father, and He is going to provide for that, then why do we ask for it?"

Here is how I answer that question: The most genuine motivation to pray is not to get something from God, but to get more *of* God. The entire Lord's Prayer is immersed in our experiencing more of our good, good Father.

Our ability to be able to speak to Him is enough. Our ability to have a relationship with Him is enough. If He chooses to provide for us in a very physical, tangible way, that is just extra. That is just the cherry on top at that point.

Our motivation to pray is not to see what we can get from Him today, treating God like the genie that you keep in your pocket. The motivation is to be able to experience more of who He is.

Our motivation to pray is not to get something from God, but it is to get more of God.

We want to be able to lavish in His character of being a provider, being all-sufficient, faithful, and true. Let's read the entire Lord's Prayer again.

> Our Father who is in heaven,
> hallowed be your name.
> Your kingdom come,
> your will be done,
> on earth as it is in heaven.
> Give us this day our daily bread,
> and forgive us our debts,
> as we also have forgiven our debtors.
> And lead us not into temptation,
> but deliver us from evil.'
> For Yours is the kingdom,
> the power and the glory,
> for ever and ever.
> Amen.

DISCUSSION

1. Are you more likely to pray using "me" or "us"? How does praying "we/our/us" keep our prayers from being selfish?

2. Read Matthew 6:25-34. How does this passage challenge your desire to be "self-reliant" for your wants and needs?

3. Because Matthew 6:11 has a communal component, what are some practical ways you could practice generosity with the resources God has given you?

4. Financial debt is a burden. Discuss why this is dangerous and how it impacts the family.

5. Discuss how our sin is also a debt to God, and read Matthew 6:12 to see Jesus' thoughts.

6. If we have been forgiven, why is it important to offer forgiveness to others?

FORGIVE

D o you have a credit card, and do you use it? I realize there are differing opinions around that, depending upon what personal finance principles you have studied.

For example, our church teaches and promotes Dave Ramsey's *Financial Peace University*, which is about getting out of debt. Or you may be like most Americans. According to the Federal Reserve, the average American family carries a credit card debt of $5,700 with them.

That can be painful and can negatively impact life. I have experienced the weight of heavy debt, and I can testify that it is painful. It is restrictive, costly, and not fun.

But you may ask, "Ricky, I thought we were studying the Lord's Prayer. What does this have to do with anything?" Just hold on, you will see. Regardless of your personal financial decision or your personal view on credit card debt, there is a concept that I think we can understand related to that, which comes into the text for this chapter.

Similar to credit card debt, there is the reality of what is called a sin debt, and that sin debt is much more costly, much

more significant. In fact, it will cost us everything. Let's read
Matthew 6:12.

*And forgive us our debts, as we also have forgiven our
debtors.*

These words are significant and carry weight. Jesus could
have used the word *sin* here, and it still would have been under-
standable. But instead, He chose to use the word *debt* perhaps
because it gives us the weight and the depth to help understanding the idea of sin.

Recognize Your Need

The first idea I want to point out in the text is to recognize
your need. Now, I realize you may have never done this before,
but you may know someone who has.

Maybe you know that there is some outstanding debt, and
you are a little bit behind on it. You get that letter in the mail,
and you choose to just leave it on the counter and not open it
because in the back of your mind, you think, *If I don't see it, I
can pretend it's not there.*

In reality is, that is only making it compound and get worse,
right? But there is this refusal to recognize the problem, which
does not really help you to gain any traction on it.

When we talk about our sin debt, we have to recognize and acknowledge it. Regardless of your income-to-debt ratio regarding your finances, all of humanity is on the same playing field when it comes to our sin debt that we have with God. Our sin is considered a debt to God.

It is a debt that we owe and have failed to eliminate. And there is a burden. In other words, you and I carry a balance with God.

Let's look at some situations that may cause this: I have done a wrong to a neighbor or to someone else's property. I have done wrong by something I've said, which damaged someone's reputation. I've exercised or exhibited pride and selfishness in my life. We could go on and on, but suffice it to say that all of us are guilty.

Here is why I think Jesus wants us to understand this analogy of our sin being debt: That sin account is entered onto God's books. It increases and can never be discharged. It can never be transferred to someone else. It cannot be escaped by the passage of years or a change of residence. I cannot file for bankruptcy to wipe out that debt or apply for a loan forgiveness program. I cannot serve enough underprivileged communities to cancel it. It is there, and payment *will* be made.

Isn't this encouraging? Don't you feel so uplifted?

We need to soak in that pain for a minute. We, as individuals, need to recognize our sin as a debt that is costly, and this debt cannot be canceled by good works. It cannot be wiped out by serving enough. I cannot give enough money on the positive side to tip the scales to the negative side.

It is solely by the grace of God offering forgiveness of this debt through the shed blood of Jesus that it can be eliminated. Here are some Scripture verses that are likely familiar to you, but let them settle in your mind:

Romans 3:23-24 For all have sinned and fallen short of the glory of God and are justified by His grace as a gift through the redemption that is in Christ Jesus.

Romans 6:23 For the wages or the consequences of sin is death. But the free gift of God is eternal life through Jesus Christ, our Lord.

Remember Pastor Frank Bowden's chapter on the petition of our daily bread? Our daily bread emphasizes our most urgent physical need, and forgiveness of our sin emphasizes our most urgent spiritual need.

We are saying that we owe a debt to God that we have failed to pay and cannot pay. Therefore, as a sinner, I stand condemned before God, fully deserving of His wrath, death, and separation forever in Hell.

How is that sitting? Heavy, I hope. I hope that it sits heavy because we must recognize our need and realize that *only* God's forgiveness can clear our guilt and establish a meaningful relationship between us and Himself. Of this verse in the Lord's Prayer, Dr. Albert Mohler said:

"This petition reminds us that the Lord's Prayer is not a casual prayer for the generically religious. This is a Gospel prayer. And we can only say these words and ask these things of God when we stand confidently on the finished, atoning work of Christ. Indeed, this petition, this prayer demonstrates that this is a theological bedrock of the Lord's Prayer. And you and I, we can rightly and confidently pray this Lord's prayer when we recognize the depth of our sin and recognize that it is only the grace of God that can remedy our souls." [8]

Feel the weight, but at the same time, feel the promise. You and I have hope today! There is a debt that is heavy and that we have to recognize... but we have hope!

Consider the story of the prodigal son. I am not going to tell you the whole story; it is in Luke 15. The short, abbreviated version is, there was a son who wanted his inheritance early. He asked that of his father, and his father gave it to him. He leaves the house, squanders it, and lives in selfishness and sin.

He sows his wild oats and satisfies every urge of his flesh. He then finds himself destitute, poor, broken, and starving. In his recognition of his need, he stands up and goes back to his home. There, his father stands ready, runs out to meet him, wraps his arms around him, forgives him, throws a party for him, and helps this prodigal son understand his identity as his child.

The father paints a mirror image of the deep love of God for us. Just like the story of the father illustrating this in *The Prodigal Son*, God the Father has sent His Son, Jesus, to rescue you, to ransom you, and to die on your behalf. And He has paid what you could not pay for your sin by His blood.

As a child of God, your sin debt has been paid; it has been satisfied. And it is in that truth that you and I can have hope. We have been ransomed from death. Our feet have been set on a rock, and I can have confidence now about what is next in Heaven. Praise God for that!

We have the beautiful privilege of putting our trust in Jesus. Perhaps you are recognizing the weight of your sin for the first time, and you have never put your trust in Jesus and walked into that relationship. You, by faith, can put trust in Him today and experience that beautiful freedom that only comes from Him.

Regenerated People Still Sin

Second, we need to understand that regenerated people still sin. What I mean by the word *regenerated* is, I once was dead in sin but now I am alive in Christ. 2 Corinthians 5 says:

> *If any man is in Christ, he is a new creation. The old has gone, the new has come.*

Even as someone who has been made new in Jesus, I still sin. I put my trust in Jesus as a child on April 12, 1984, to be specific. I understood the Gospel as much as I could at that age. I recognized my need, put my faith in Jesus, and I was made new. It was *after* that exchange that I was consumed by anger, doubted the faithfulness of God, and walked through a season of addiction to pornography. --*after* my soul was forever changed.

Why? Because as a regenerated soul, I still sin... and so do you. Just as I needed to recognize my sin, I need to rest in the reality that if it were not for the forgiveness of God, I would be hopeless.

Notice that this is following right after the daily bread section. Life without forgiveness would not be worth having. It is the shed blood of Jesus that was a one-time payment that satisfied the debt that I owed to God for all the sin in my past, my present, and my future.

In fact, the Greek word used for forgiveness here in the text and throughout the New Testament literally could be translated with this idea of letting go or releasing someone from obligation. This means because of my sin, I earned death. That is what I deserved. But because I am forgiven, I am released from that obligation. Thank you, Jesus!

But even though I am forgiven, even though I am in Christ made new, I still sin. I think that is what Jesus was trying to teach His disciples in John 13:10. He worded it this way:

One who is bathed does not need to wash except the feet, but is entirely clean.

The image that Jesus is trying to give us and help us understand is, you have been made new. You have been washed clean. That is not something you need to repeat.

But you are going to continue to walk through dirty roads in the muck and mire of life, and your feet will continually be dirty. As a regenerated soul, I am going to continue to sin, but that does not require me to go back and get saved all over again.

That was a *one-time* payment for my sin. It was the death, burial and resurrection of Jesus. It is His shed blood and finished work that allows me to be saved. It is the promised seal of the Holy Spirit that perseveres and keeps me. But, I still need to continually walk in His forgiveness because my feet get dirty.

This is a statement of our identity. This is a statement of the confidence that you and I can carry throughout life. We do not have to walk throughout this life with shame and guilt over things we have done in the past. You and I can walk in freedom over the captivity of sin in our lives.

Martin Luther said it this way: "Believers in this life are at the same time righteous and sinner."[9] As children of God, you and I stand forgiven, but not perfect. That is not an expectation. We pursue righteousness and strive to become more like Jesus.

It is important that we remember that our brothers and sisters in our faith family are not perfect either. Even though we love each other, we are going to fail. We are going to hurt each other's feelings. We are going to say things that bother or offend each other. But we love each other and heal through that.

However, our forgiveness does not give us a license to go and do whatever we want. I am reminded of a friend of mine. Once on a Friday as we were about to leave for the weekend, I asked, "Hey, what have you got going on this weekend? What are you going to do?" She said, "I don't know what you're going to do, but I'm going to go get plastered drunk this weekend. That's my plan."

I said, "What? Why would you do that? And why would you *plan* for that?" She said, "Oh, it's no big deal because I'll just go to church on Sunday and ask Jesus to forgive me. It's fine."

She was missing a really important part of this equation. Romans 6:1-2 says:

What shall we say then? Are we to continue in sin so that grace may abound? By no means.

Or your translation may say, "God forbid that I would do that, that I would abuse that love and grace and mercy of God in that way." 2 Corinthians 5:21 says:

For our sake, He made Him to be sin who knew no sin, so that in Him, we might become the righteousness of God.

As a child of God, my pursuit should be striving to every day be more like Him and to allow Him to influence my choices and behavior. I want Him to influence my actions, and I do not want to abuse His grace to get me to go serve every selfish urge that I have. You see the difference.

At the end of the day, this should impact how we live. At the end of the day, this should impact how we pray. How we understand the Gospel and how we appreciate what God has done for us impacts our identity. Our understanding of Him influences the confidence that we can come to Him as Father in prayer and make any petition to Him.

This impacts our self-worth and our relationships with others. Our position in Christ *must* impact how we treat people.

My position in Christ must impact how I treat people.

We cannot avoid that because of the second half of Matthew 6:12. Look at what it says:

Forgive us our debts, as we also have forgiven our debtors.

Reconciled People Forgive

Reconciled people forgive. Reconciled people are those of us who are believers and have been made right with God. We have been reconciled, bought back, and thus, we should forgive. God's forgiveness is not contingent on my ability to forgive, but this illustrates that the same level of forgiveness we have experienced from God, we should extend to others.

In other words, this is a gift with expectation. It is so significant, in fact, that when Jesus finished teaching the Lord's Prayer in Matthew 6, as soon as you get to verses 14 and 15, He jumps right back into forgiveness again. Forgiving others is that significant.

Martin Luther King, Jr. said, "The old law of 'an eye for an eye' leaves everybody blind."[10] Furthermore, Ephesians 4:32 lays out this expectation for how we should live:

Be kind one to another, tender-heartedly, forgiving one another as God in Christ has forgiven you.

Forgiven people ought to forgive. It is a divine investment with a challenge to carry out a ministry of forgiveness and reconciliation. The heart of this reality, then, should strive for me to have healthy relationships.

Forgiven people ought to forgive.

It should motivate me to reconcile a broken marriage, to strive to restore a wounded relationship between a child and a parent, to work to rebuild longstanding divisions over race and ethnicity. This ministry of reconciliation, as Paul defines it, has been given to the church, and it should change our perspective toward others.

We have two little yappers, two little maltipoos. One is five pounds and one is nine pounds. Some call them dogs; you may call them bait. One of the things that we find humorous is, sometimes they are playing, and they start chasing their tails. Have you ever seen a dog do this? It is really cute and funny.

But when you and I are unwilling to forgive, it causes the relationship to continually run in a circle like a dog chasing its tail. Not forgiving and running this cycle in a relationship is not funny. In fact, it is painful.

It causes a marriage relationship to continually repeat the same argument over a past offense over and over again. It causes a child to resist trusting his or her parents because at one point in life, that trust was broken, and it recycles pain. An unwillingness to forgive creates a whirlwind of hurt, rather than a spring of hope. This is hard.

C.S. Lewis even said it this way: "It is perhaps not so hard to forgive a great injury. But to forgive incessant provocations of daily life, to keep on forgiving the bossy mother-in-law, the bullying husband, the nagging wife, the selfish daughter, the deceitful son, how can we do it?"[11]

C.S. Lewis is a lot smarter than I am, so let me put this in Ricky language. I may be more prone to forgive the person at the grocery store who said something that bothered me than I am the people I live with. That is sad, but true.

Forgiveness is hard when we have been wounded by the actions of another, but just because it is hard does not give us a pass. Jesus going to the cross was hard, and I am thankful that He did not take a pass on that. I cannot view a person based upon his or her actions in the past. I must view that person through the eyes of Christ, as someone who is loved, who is worthy enough for God to send His son to die for, and someone whom God desires to have a relationship with.

We used *The Prodigal Son* earlier, but let's use another illustration from the book of Jonah. Hopefully you are familiar with the story. If not, it is only four chapters long.

Jonah was a prophet of God. God had given a command for him to go to the city of Nineveh to prophesy, but he had a really big issue with Nineveh and didn't want to go. He tried to run away from God, so he went in the complete opposite direction.

He gets in a shipwreck, gets thrown overboard, and a big fish swallows Him up. While he is in the belly of this big fish for three days and nights, he has a change of heart. He repents, recognizes his sin, and the fish spits him out on dry land. He goes to Nineveh, delivers the message that God had sent Him with, and the people of Nineveh changed their hearts.

In chapter four with Jonah on top of the hill looking down over the city, he showed that even though he obeyed God, his view toward the people of Nineveh had not changed. He still wanted them to burn.

I think the most significant point of the book of Jonah is not the obedience of Jonah, though that is what we recognize. The last verse in the last chapter is perhaps the most significant part of the story when God speaks. This is what He says in Jonah 4:11:

Should I not be concerned about Nineveh, that great city in which there are more than 120,000 persons who do not know their right hand from their left and also many animals?

It is as if God is saying to Jonah, "Look at that city. If you saw them the way that I see them, you would only reach one conclusion. It is worth it."

Our hearts should break for our sin. Our hearts should break for our family, for a city and neighbors who desperately need to experience the forgiveness of Jesus. Oh, that we would see our neighbors and our community through the eyes of God! We, like Him, would say, "They are worth it."

If I had the capacity to go one by one and pay off the credit card and mortgage and student loan debt of every person reading this book, I would do it in a heartbeat, because the freedom of that financial impact would have a ripple impact on the community of the Kingdom of God. It would be exponential and beautiful.

But I don't. I don't have that ability. However, I have news that is even better than that. What I do have is hope for everyone. I have the hope of the debt that our sin deserves and the weight of eternity being separated from God is wiped out because of the shed blood of Jesus.

Jesus died on the cross. His body was broken and poured out for you, and this single, one act changed history forever. It changed my life when I put my trust in Him. I pray that you can reconcile that and walk and live in that level of confidence, walking in freedom over the guilt that sin may bring on you from your past.

I pray that you will allow this truth to change you today, change how you view yourself, change how you view others, and change how you pray. To that end, let's all pray together. Let's say the Lord's Prayer again.

Our Father who is in heaven,
hallowed be your name.
Your kingdom come,
your will be done,
on earth as it is in heaven.
Give us this day our daily bread,
and forgive us our debts,
as we also have forgiven our debtors.
And lead us not into temptation,
but deliver us from evil.'
For Yours is the kingdom,
the power and the glory,
for ever and ever.
Amen.

DISCUSSION

1. Read Matthew 6:12, and discuss how our sin and actions compare to a debt.

2. How does a forgiven sin debt impact our view of God, self, and others?

3. Why are we sometimes unwilling to forgive others when we have been wronged?

4. Think about times in your life when you have faced trials and temptations. What are some differences between ones leading to sin and ones leading to character?

5. Read 1 Corinthians 10:13-15. What does this tell us about temptation?

6. What do you think the purpose of temptation or trials in our life are? Why would God lead us into them? See Matthew 6:13.

TEMPTATION

This whole time, we have been learning to more active-ly engage in prayer and to use the Lord's Prayer as a model to build off of. That was Jesus's intention. In this chapter, we come to Matthew 6:13.

Now, to set the stage, lately, I have been doing more baking, and I recently made some cookies. When we think about tempta-tion, sometimes we hear that word, and we think of food, be-cause let's just be honest; for many of us, food can be tempting.

For me personally, I do not claim to have a sweet tooth, but I will unapologetically say chocolate chip cookies are my down-fall. If I were on a cruise and a massive buffet of every dessert known to man was there, I would look for the chocolate chip cookies and go straight to them.

Not to be arrogant, but I think I have enough willpower that I could resist a piece of cake or a piece of pie, even though I love those things. But a chocolate chip cookie, I just cannot resist. And sadly, I generally cannot just eat one.

This, for many of us, is an understanding of the idea behind temptation. We get this because we have all been tempted to eat too much or go a little too far.

That is a picture of what temptation can be. However, what we will see in this chapter is that it is not a complete picture. My heart's desire as we unpack Matthew 6:13 is that you will have a little more of a well-rounded view, though it still will not be a *complete* explanation of temptation. Let's read and dive in:

And lead us not into temptation, but deliver us from evil.

This can be a really hard verse to understand, because when we read it at first pass, it probably brings a lot of questions to our minds like, "Will God lead us into temptation? Is that what this is saying? I thought He loved me.

The Reality of Temptation

Let me begin with this: Temptation is real. Every one of us, at some point in our lives (perhaps even every day) deals with the knock of temptation on our heart's desire. It could be to take something that is not ours, to stretch the truth to make ourselves appear better than we are, to lust after someone, or to hatch a scheme so that we can selfishly get our way.

Even the sincerest and most well-intentioned believers struggle daily with the temptation to please the flesh, please the eye, and walk in pride. This is a part of the life that we have to navigate, and we wrestle with our sin nature constantly.

We know that there is the reality of temptation, and *wanting* to do the right thing and *actually doing it*, are two very different things. Can you relate?

Thankfully, even the apostle Paul related to this. We see his transparent description of his internal struggle in Romans 7. He says, "Hey look, I get it. The things that I know I shouldn't do, I find myself doing all the time. And the things I know I should do, I can't motivate myself to do."

So, Paul even wrestled with the fact that there is the reality of temptation that we all face. But this verse in Matthew has some interesting language that leads to a question. It says that Jesus, praying to the Father, said "Lead us not into temptation."

This begs this question, does God tempt His people in such a way that they have to pray this prayer? Well, let's look at Scripture. There is no better way to filter hard questions in life than to ask, what does God's Word say? Look at James 1: 13-15:

Let no one say when he is tempted, I'm being tempted by God. For God cannot be tempted with evil and he himself tempts no one.

I am forced into a little bit of quandary at first glance. On the one hand, I read in James 1 that God will not tempt anybody. And then I read in Matthew 6, "God, don't lead me into temptation." Either I have just discovered a contradiction in Scripture or perhaps there is a need for me to make sure I study and understand what is being said here.

Here is the reality: James 1 clearly describes the nature of God in that He is not going to tempt you to do evil. God Himself would never tempt us. But He *will* allow us to be tempted.

Consider the story of Job. It begins with this supernatural dialogue between God and the Evil One. The Devil is approaching God, saying, "Who can I go after?" And God permits Satan to go after and tempt Job.

When it comes to that tribulation, we might say, "Well, who was responsible?" Satan did the act of temptation, but God allowed it to happen so that Job could be tested.

For most of us, our view of temptation is limited to this definition. We see temptation only as a gateway to sin and disobedience or the stepping stone toward sin. While yes, that may be true, that is not complete. In fact, I hope to broaden your understanding a little bit so you see that temptation actually can be for your good.

Temptation Leads to Endurance

Let me give you a couple of points and Scripture verses. First, temptation leads us to endurance in our faith. 1 Corinthians 10:13 says:

No temptation has overtaken you that is not common to man. God is faithful and he will not let you be tempted beyond your ability, but with the temptation, he will also provide the way of escape, that you may be able to endure it.

There is a purpose and benefit to strengthen your spiritual endurance by navigating temptation.

Temptation Reveals Character

The second way temptation can be good is, it reveals your character. In other words, temptation may expose some areas of your life that you have not surrendered to the authority of God. Look at Romans 5:1-5 :

Therefore, since we have been justified by faith, we have peace with God through our Lord Jesus Christ. Through him, we have also obtained access by faith into this grace in which we stand. And we rejoice in the hope of the glory of God. Not only that, but we rejoice in our suffering, knowing that suffering produces endurance, and endurance produces character, and character produces hope, and hope does not put us to shame, because God's love has been poured into our hearts through the Holy Spirit who has been given to us.

Temptation Weeds Out Hypocrisy

Furthermore, temptation weeds out hypocrisy. James 1:14-15 says:

But each person is tempted when he is lured and enticed by his own desire. Then desire when it has conceived, gives birth to sin, and sin, when it is fully grown, brings forth death.

Temptation does not equal sin. If it did, we would not have a perfect Jesus, because Jesus experienced temptation. Temptation will weed out and expose some hypocrisy in your life so you can see, "Wow! I didn't realize I had those rough edges that need to be refined and sanded down by the potter."

Temptations from God will demonstrate our character and highlight our faith. They will reveal our trust and reveal blind spots. They will reveal and expose weaknesses in our hearts.

But they also build endurance. They transform our view of God. They mold us prayerfully into His image, and they shape our relationship with God and man. Temptations are allowed from God for our good, and they reflect the heart of a loving God who desires to see you and me transformed into the image of His Son.

Temptation in and of itself is not designed to make us fall. Temptation is designed to make us stronger and better men and women, stronger followers of Jesus, and stronger in our faith. Temptation is not designed to make us sin; it is designed to help us be good and more like Him.

For example, let's go back to this analogy of cookies. Let's say I really try to watch my calorie intake, and I track everything I eat. Well, when I have reached my intake for the day, and chocolate chip cookies are still on the counter, now I am dealing with a temptation factor. Am I going to please myself, or am I going to have a successful moment to resist so that I can stay true to my goals for the day?

So, it is helping me grow, because when I resist and have that victory, the next time, hopefully it is a little easier to maintain that level of discipline. Again, temptation does not equal sin, and it is not so much the penalty for being human as it is the glory of being human. It is much more than just a gateway to sin; there are some benefits to it.

At the end of the day, this is all a simple game of Follow the Leader. God Himself may test his children, but He does not tempt them. Instead, He helps His own children, and in fact, the Greek word used here in Matthew 6:13 for temptation is the exact same Greek word used for testing, and it also carries that meaning.

For example, Paul tells the Corinthian church, "Put yourself to the test (same word as temptation) to see if you are in the faith. Examine yourselves (2 Corinthians 13:5)."

Again, temptation is not simply a gateway to sin; it is a test of my faith. Am I going to follow God in this moment?

The notion that God would tempt us to sin is a theological problem. The reality that God may test His people to prove their faith is encouraging. Proverbs 17:3 says this:

The crucible for refining silver and the furnace is for gold. Likewise, the Lord tests hearts.

Evaluate your life. Where is God testing you? Charles Spurgeon was a pretty smart guy, and this is what he said: "Full often, the great captain of salvation leads us by his providence to battlefields, where we must face the fell array of evil and conquer through the blood of the lamb and this leading into temptation is by divine grace, overruled for our good, since by being tempted, we go strong in grace and patience."[12]

Follow the Leader

This is a game of Follow the Leader, and the encouragement for us is that Jesus told us, "I am never going to leave you. I will always be with you. And even more so, I have gone before you. I am moving ahead of you. I am fighting your battles on your behalf. And (specifically related to temptation) I am not putting you through any tests that I have not walked through myself." That is an incredible encouragement for us.

When we read of Jesus' temptation for 40 days in the wilderness, when He was pressed in on every side as He was tested, we see Him praying the spirit of Matthew 6:13, in the Garden of Eden.

Remember, He is lamenting and laboring over this path that the Father is pushing Him through. And He says, "If it is your will, God, let this cup pass from me. Nevertheless, not my will, but yours be done."

In that moment, He was demonstrating for us the power of walking through a test where your will is being pressed against the will of God. Are you willing to submit and surrender through that? God puts His people through a process of refinement for the sake of growth and maturity.

Let me use a very simple, earthly example to illustrate the point. Almost every year, I try to go to New York on a mission trip. When I go, part of that mission experience is serving the community and engaging with people in parks, and talking to them about Jesus has been wonderful.

The last several years, I have been able to take my daughters with me, and they have been able to experience this. There is no more joy than being on a mission trip with your kids and watching them step out of their comfort zone and carry on Gospel conversations with total strangers. It is beautiful.

But there is also a layer of benefit as a father to teach them some life skills. Three years ago, on this specific trip, I was leading a group in New York for a week, and I was facilitating for another church. I try to be very intentional with my girls about learning how to navigate the streets, what to watch for, signs of things that are unsafe, things you want to avoid, looking ahead down the path, how to navigate the subway, how to transfer from one train to the other, and get back to the hotel.

I had navigated for them and had demonstrated for them. Finally, at about three days in, I said, "Okay Ladies, this is your test. You have got to get this youth group back to the hotel, and I will lag in the distance."

They were nervous and fearful, but they did it like champs. They navigated the team to safety. They got them on the right subway, transferred from the right train, got off at the right stop, all the way to the hotel lobby. They did a great job.

Now, why do I tell you that story? That is an example of me as a father having demonstrated for them how to do it, but then getting them to a place to say, "Now is the time for you to pass the test. I've shown you the way; I've modeled for you what to do, but now you must be tested to see if you actually get it, can navigate it, and can be obedient to it."

That is much like life for us. In this game of Follow the Leader, God has demonstrated for us. Jesus has modeled for us. He has shown us the way. But there comes a point where we have to say, "Okay Lord, I realize that you are now testing me to see if I am going to put in action and what you have demonstrated for me."

That is a moment that we often call temptation. The prayer to not be led into temptation is not a desire to necessarily circumvent or get away from the trials that God has set before us. This prayer or petition is not intended to then make us lazy in our faith. Rather, it marks an appeal of a trusting child to remain with their father, whatever the outcome might be as we follow the leader.

Be Delivered From Temptation

Now we get to the second half of the verse, though, which is to be delivered from temptation. Let's read the second half again of Matthew 6:13:

But deliver us from evil.

Truthfully, a more accurate translation would say, "But deliver us from the Evil One." That word there is really a proper noun describing that we have an enemy around us, and he is active. Lest you think we do not have an enemy, lest you think he is not active, just pause for a minute, and look around you. We are reminded every day of the evil that exists and of the Evil One who is at work.

In fact, there are two points I would like to make here. One is, this Evil One, the Enemy, Satan is working to destroy the world and he is active in doing so. We know that God's Word tells us that we have an enemy who is like a roaring lion, roaming to and fro, seeking whom he may devour (1 Peter 5:8).

The early church understood and even adopted the words of Matthew 24, that the end of times will be marked by evil. We see it today in wars across the world, pestilence (which is another word for a pandemic), divisions where there should be unity, senseless murders in the streets, murders in the womb at abortion clinics, corruption in the government, injustice in our systems, religious freedoms that are in jeopardy today, rampant crime in the street, fundamental restructuring of marriage and family and gender. The Evil One is active around us.

If you do not see it, you have got your head in the sand.

What do we do about it? Some days, if we are being really honest, we look around our world and it feels like the enemy is winning. But God is stirring in His Church that we do not relent. Instead we need to repent. God is calling the Church to awaken. God is calling the Church to recognize that in Him, we are more than conquerors.

God is our deliverer and He is not done with the Church. We must not relent. In fact, I am just naively optimistic enough to think that He is stirring a new work in His Church right now. The Evil One makes widespread progress when he consistently wins at the individual level.

The Enemy is working to destroy the world, but more importantly, he is working to destroy you. And you must recognize it. You must see it and be aware of it. Pray like the words here. "Deliver us, oh God! Rescue us, oh God!"

In my nature, I cannot overcome the Evil One, but in Christ, I have victory. And in that moment of temptation, there is a way of escape promised for me. Let's go back and reread 1 Corinthians 10:13-15:

> *No temptation has overtaken you that is not common to man. God is faithful and he will not let you be tempted beyond your ability. But with the temptation, he will also provide the way of escape. That you may be able to endure it.*

There is an imagery here of a platoon of soldiers trapped in a rugged country, and then they see a passageway through the hills to escape. They may have thought they were pinned in, but all of a sudden, a route has opened up for escape. God has promised you every single time in those moments of testing and temptation, there is a way of escape for you.

That way of escape may be relocating the computer out of that private room and into a place where everybody can see. That way of escape may be you putting that cell phone down before you say something you shouldn't. That way of escape may be you calling out for accountability from someone else, because you know, when you are put in a certain situation, you are going to stumble. He is always providing those ways of escape, if we have the courage to see it.

The Devil tempts men, that he may destroy them. God tests men, that the chaff may be separated and sifted, or the dross may be burned away in the refiner's fire with the ultimate aim that we demonstrate a more pure reflection of His glory to the world.

He leads us into and through battles for our good. In other words, as Charles Spurgeon has said, "God tempts men for probation, but never for perdition."[13]

> ### God tempts men for PROBATION, but never for PERDITION.

Now, let me say that a different way, because those are words that we do not commonly use in our language. God allows temptation for your testing, but never for your destruction. God will allow situations and trials, tribulations, and tests to come into your life to test your faith. But, they are never to destroy you.

You may be hearing all of this and thinking, "Okay. So what?"

Let me give you three really practical thoughts. The first one is this: Believers should recognize that they are part of an ongoing spiritual battle. Read Ephesians 6 beginning in verse 10:

We wrestle not against flesh and blood.

There is a spiritual battle at play against evil forces in this world. You cannot see it, but it directly impacts the world that you *can* see. Acknowledge that we are in a fight for our minds, for our families, and for our faith.

Second, believers should recognize that evil forces are very clever. You see, I am never tempted to have a chocolate chip cookie at 11:00 in the morning. I am tempted to have a chocolate chip cookie at 11:00 at night, when it is the worst for me.

He is clever, because he knows where your weaknesses are, and the Evil One is going to introduce those temptations when you are most likely to fail. So, be careful with your pride. About the time you think you have whipped whatever it is, he is going to bite you.

Third, the assumption behind the Lord's Prayer is that believers can only withstand temptations and the forces of evil by staying connected closely to the Father and relying on His power and mercy. Let's get really practical with what that looks like. You must stay closely connected to the Lord through prayer, through the studying of His Word, through community with other believers, because there is strength in those moments.

If you are not staying closely connected to the Father, do not be surprised when you lose the temptation game. Do not be shocked when the test comes your way, and you fail over and over again. It is important that we follow the leader, that we stay closely connected to the Father and rely on His grace.

It is through that relationship, through prayer and falling in love with His Word that He equips us and teaches us who we are in Him. More importantly, who He is as our King.

I know that route sounds really simple. I realize it is more complicated than that. But that is a root-level discipline that has a significant impact on your faith every day.

That being said, let's pray the Lord's Prayer one more time.

> Our Father who is in heaven,
> hallowed be your name.
> Your kingdom come,
> your will be done,
> on earth as it is in heaven.
> Give us this day our daily bread,
> and forgive us our debts,
> as we also have forgiven our debtors.
> And lead us not into temptation,
> but deliver us from evil.'
> For Yours is the kingdom,
> the power and the glory,
> for ever and ever. Amen.

He is good. He is our Father. We can trust Him. Even when we walk through the pain of testing, we can trust Him. He will never leave us, nor forsake us.

DISCUSSION

1. Read Matthew 4:1-11. How was Jesus tempted, and how did he escape?

2. Based on Jesus' example, how can we escape temptation when it comes?

3. In the Lord's Prayer, it says *US*. Why is that important , and what does it mean for Christian living?

REVIEW

In the beginning of this book, I stated that prayer is our lifeline and communication in a real relationship. Therefore, it is vital for us to practice it and get comfortable with talking to God in good times and bad. Thankfully, we were not left on our own to figure out how to do it. God Himself, the second person of the Trinity, Jesus Christ, came here and said, "Pray in this way…"

Chapter One was an introduction to the Lord's Prayer. We talked about how prayer is not just asking God for things like He is a genie in a bottle. Prayer is how God molds us into being more like Him, not us making Him do things.

We also said that in prayer, keep it simple; don't feel like you have to be long-winded to try to impress God. The Lord's Prayer is simply laid out. It is not a mantra to be mindlessly repeated. Rather, it is a model, or skeleton we can use to focus our thoughts.

Chapter Two was the beginning of really getting into the prayer itself. Remember to start by acknowledging God and who He is, not by running down a list of requests. Slow down, first acknowledging Him as our heavenly Father who loves you. With other relationships, you would not start by jumping into requests and not recognizing the person to whom you are speaking.

Also, His name is holy and should be treated as such. When we say, "Hallowed be thy name," we remember that we are speaking to the Lord of lords and the respect with which we should speak.

In Chapter Three, Dr. Samuel Thomas discussed how difficult it is to give up your will to another. To honestly say, "Thy will be done," is one of the hardest prayers to pray. It means you do not doubt that God intends the best for you, even if the best involves pain and suffering. It reflects absolute trust and is so difficult because it is the opposite of what the world stands for. But if you do it, God can use you in amazing ways.

Chapter Four was about God's provision. Frank Bowden talked about how, when it IS time to ask for things in your prayers, we never have to worry that God will get tired us our asking. In fact, He loves it when we come to Him like a child coming to his or her parents. This does not mean that He will give us whatever we want, but sometimes we have not because we ask not (James 4:2-3).

Frank also reminded us that God provides for us day by day, and He has promised to provide for *all* of our needs. When you ask God to provide for you today, it is an act of worship. It is a way of showing you trust that He can provide, and it is a way of experiencing more of Him.

In Chapter Five was about the heavy weight of debt and the freedom of forgiveness. Our sin is a debt that we cannot pay off. You cannot do enough good works to get rid of it.

But, praise be to God that He loves us so much that He paid that debt for us! He is like the father in the story of *The Prodigal Son*. Believers who have trusted in Christ are free, right with God, and our sin debt is forgiven. However, that does not mean that you will not continue to sin. We still have to battle with our sin nature until we die, but we have a cancelled debt and our eternity is secure in Heaven.

And because we have been completely forgiven, we are commanded to forgive others. Sometimes this is not easy, but if you think about *how much* you have been forgiven and how much you did not deserve it, forgiving others becomes easier.

Finally, Chapter Six addressed the topic of temptation. Remember, God does not tempt us to do evil, but He sometimes allows us to be tempted. And, temptation is not altogether a bad thing. It can lead to endurance, it reveals your character, and weeds out hypocrisy.

When you are tempted, follow Jesus' example and overcome it with Scripture. He always provides a way out, and He does not abandon us. Temptation will come, and it can test you and strengthen you; it does not have to destroy you. When we say in the Lord's Prayer, "Deliver us from the Evil One," we are acknowledging that God really can deliver us, and it shows that we are relying on Him to give us strength.

The whole goal of this book has been to deepen your prayer life by giving confidence when you approach God. Jesus gave you a structure for prayer, so you don't have to worry about not having anything to say. You can easily begin where Jesus said to begin...with "Our Father".

Then, just keep it simple, moving from acknowledgement, to submitting to God's will, to asking for provision, to seeing where you need forgiveness and where you need to forgive others, to strength through temptation.

If this book has helped you, I would love to know about it. Or if you would like to know more about beginning a relationship with God through Jesus Chris, I would love to talk to you about that, too. Contact me at: ricky@calvaryga.com

REFERENCES

[1]Bernstein, E. (2020, May 17). The Science of Prayer. *WSJ*. https://www.wsj.com/articles/the-science-of-prayer-11589720400

[2]Martin Luther. *A Simple Way to Pray*. (Louisville: Westminster John Knox Press, 2000), p.34.

[3]Ritchie, G. (Director). (2019). *Aladdin* [Film]. Walt Disney Pictures.

[4]Wachowski, L and L. (Directors). (1999). *The Matrix* [Film]. Warner Bros.

[5]Lewis, C. S. (2015). *The Great Divorce* (Revised ed.). HarperOne.

[6]Brainard, Mary. "I Know Not What Awaits Me." *hymn (1869)*. https://hymnary.org/text/i_know_not_what_awaits_me_-god_kindly

[7]Tomlin, Chris. "Good Good Father." *Never Lose Sight* album (2016).

[8]Mohler, Albert. (2018, November 29). "'Forgive Us Our Debts': The Lord's Prayer Is A Gospel Prayer". https://albert-mohler.com/2018/11/29/forgive-us-debts-lords-prayer-gospel-prayer

[9]Bingham, Nathan. (2019, October 17). "What Does 'Simul Justus et Peccator' Mean?" https://www.ligonier.org/blog/simul-justus-et-peccator/

[10]King, Jr., Martin Luther. https://www.brainyquote.com/quotes/martin_luther_king_jr_387472

[11]C.S. Lewis, *The Weight of Glory* (New York: Simon & Schuster, 1996), pp. 135-136.

[12]Spurgeon, Charles. "Lead Us Not Into Temptation", a sermon delivered on May 17, 1863. https://www.ccel.org/ccel/spurgeon/sermons09.xxiii.html

[13]Spurgeon, Charles. "Lead Us Not Into Temptation", a sermon delivered on May 17, 1863. https://www.ccel.org/ccel/spurgeon/sermons09.xxiii.html

ABOUT THE AUTHORS

Ricky Smith is currently the lead pastor of Calvary Baptist Church in Columbus, Georgia and provides leadership to the multi-faceted ministry with a commitment to make disciples in the Chattahoochee Valley and to the ends of the earth. Ricky's ministry career has been focused on making the name of Jesus known and advancing the mission of the Gospel.

He received a bachelor's degree in Christian Education with an emphasis in Youth Ministry from Bryan College. He holds a Masters degree in Theology from Liberty Baptist Seminary, and he holds a Specialist Degree in Educational Leadership from Liberty University. He also holds an honorary doctorate from Emmanuel Theological Seminary.

Follow Ricky on social media using @rickylamarsmith.

Dr. Samuel Thomas, born in 1967, is known throughout India as a leading humanitarian. Following in the footsteps of his father, Dr. M. A. Thomas, Founder of Hopegivers International, Dr. Samuel is a second generation visionary for the organization.

Dr. Samuel, a dynamic leader and speaker, united with his father in the vision for "One Million Arrows" for God that continues to fuel the explosive growth of Hopegivers International throughout India and other developing nations. Their vision is to see One Million needy children rescued from brothels, slums and the streets of India, trained and sent out as Orphan Leaders Worldwide by the year 2030.

Dr. Samuel's education includes undergraduate work at Columbia International University, a B. A. from Liberty University, and a Doctorate in Divinity from Antioch Seminary. He has also received an Honorary Doctorate of Humanities from Liberty University and an Honorary Doctorate of Divinity from North Greenville University.

An accomplished singer, instrumentalist and songwriter, Dr. Samuel has recorded 15 devotional song albums in the Hindi and Malayalam languages. He conducts leadership seminars in India, the Middle East and in the United States. He is an internationally renowned conference speaker.

Dr. Samuel Thomas is married to the former Shelley Lucas from Harpswell, Maine. They have two sons, Steven Andrew and Timothy Abraham.

Frank Bowden currently serves as the Student Pastor for Calvary Baptist Church in Columbus, Georgia. Having been born and raised in the Chattahoochee Valley, his call to ministry "at home" is special for him. For over 13 years, he has pastored students and families in the Columbus area.

Frank's passion centers around this phrase: *students helping students find and follow Jesus.* He is committed to Next Gen ministry and seeing the advancement of the Gospel through students.

He received a bachelor's degree in Christian Studies from Brewton-Parker College. Frank also holds a master's degree in Apologetics from Luther Rice Seminary.

Hopegivers
INTERNATIONAL
www.hopegivers.org

Hopegivers International promotes advocacy for abandoned, and at-risk children in the nations of India, Nepal, Myanmar and Haiti. Our mission is to assist the needy and the oppressed in collaboration with our Ministry Partners. We want to educate those we rescue and give them an opportunity to impact their culture in a positive way.

Contact Info:
(866) 373-HOPE
PO Box 8808, Columbus, GA 31908
info@hopegivers.org

www.ingramcontent.com/pod-product-compliance
Lightning Source LLC
Chambersburg PA
CBHW070049040426
42331CB00034B/2636